SKINT PORTLAND
FOR THE FRUGAL VAGABOND

Skint Press | Portland, Oregon

Skint Portland is published by Skint Press
skintpress.net
PO Box 1054
1505 SW 6th Ave.
Portland, OR 97201

Publisher and Managing Editor: Mary Locke
Copy Editor: Rachel Katz, with additional editing by Grant Miller
Cover and Layout Design: Jordan Sellergren

The publisher would like to acknowledge the hard work and insight of
Kaarin Thompson, Gregg Morris, Rachel Katz, Joel Bell, Maranda Bish,
Ian Friedman, Carib Andante-Rivera, Jordan Sellergren, Cleveland Harris,
Evan Crittenden, Casey Harris, Constance and Eric Johnson, Karen Locke,
Mark Locke, Joey Haugsted, Nic Smith, Jimmy Askren, Chris Sutton,
Cresta White, Paul Cary, Emily Magnuson and Grant Miller

For Felix and Thorsten

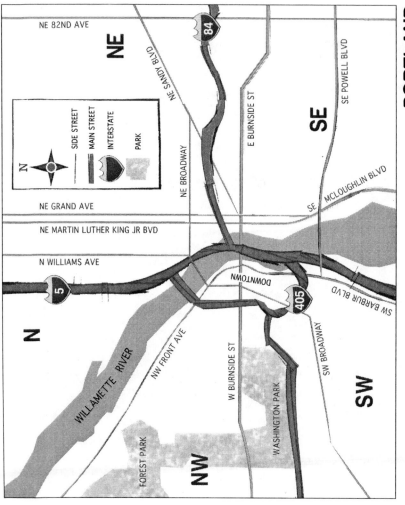

PORTLAND

contents

CHAPTER 1

INTRODUCTION

Skint Portland attempts to remove some of the shiny, liberal veneer off of its city, in order to reveal a more candid, honest experience of the town. At times Portland may seem like the caricature of an impossibly light-skinned, politically correct, sustainable utopia, but Skint Portland hopes to lessen this distortion. Portland is a complicated, beautiful city: one worth exploring. Moreover, the farther you can stretch your dollar, the longer you can stay. Skint Portland highlights the dive bars that will sate your lust for swill, diners that will get you fueled for under six dollars, and inexpensive rooms for shut-eye. Skint Portland provides a point of reference for venues, record shops, and bookstores in town, assuming the form of an honest, thrifty compass to get you where you need to go. This is the scratch-the-surface guide to get you there—cheaply.

Mary Locke, Publisher

the writers

Joel Bell

Joel Forrest Bell is 27 years old, 5'11", 180 pounds, and has yet to reproduce. He was born in Texas, and currently lives in Oregon—a difference of almost 2,000 miles!

Thanks to...

Joe and Ellen Bell, Beth Morgan, Carib Rivera Guerra, Francis and Gonzolo Garza Independence High School.

Maranda Bish

Maranda Bish is one of those rare Oregon natives roaming the adult playground of North Portland. Fame and fortune came calling early for Maranda, raised in scenic Astoria, with a role as a child extra in Scwarzenegger's master work Kindergarten Cop. Tragically, these dazzling heights could find no parallel in later years, and Maranda spiraled into a life of hedonism and squalor. She now earns her keep as a (questionable) role model for children as a teacher and a half-assed freelance writer for the Portland Mercury, Oregon Voice and others. Hobbies include being belligerent and getting parking tickets at the Indian food cart. Maranda spends a good portion of every day trying to more closely resemble a woman in a Quentin Tarantino movie, by wearing animal print, having impeccable music taste and spouting occasional witticisms.

Thanks to...

First, to my dearest friend and roommate Kelly Rulon, without whom my sanity, safety and hygiene would be even more compromised than it already is: I love you. Heartfelt gratitude to my family, who accepts, if not encourages, my wayward lifestyle—especially my beloved grandmother, Jeri "Nana" Boyle. May you rest in peace. Finally, big ups to Joey "Awesome" Haugsted, for being just that.

the writers

Ian Friedman

Ian Friedman lives in southeast Portland, where he subsists on a steady diet of bánh mì sandwiches and Irish whiskey. He's a poet and a musician, and is also a direct descendant of Poseidon. Ian can be found at Exiled Records, La Bamba, or the liquor store on Powell and 50th.

Thanks to...

All my friends and family, and Eazy-E.

Carib Andante-Rivera

Est. 1984 +41.2 -123.2; 1/6,852,472,823; loc. +40.7 -73.9 circa 2011

Thanks to...

There are a lot of people, places, and things I would list in gratitude for their support. Most of them know who they are. However, in context, my biggest thanks must go to the lowest common denominators of human society. You lazy, fair-weather, morning drunks have persevered and kept it real. Without you, a meal would be just a meal, a bathroom simply a bathroom, and every hour at a bar would be merely content. You've given us the all-you-can-eat lunch buffet, the scratched-metal-sheet-mirror in only the nicest of public toilets, and most of all, you've given us the dead-cheap drink special. These things exist because bar owners understand that you won't drink there otherwise. We've long known that "these colors don't run," but you've made it perfectly clear that the colors really don't do much at all, and for that, you deserve our thanks. You are the U.S. of America.

Mary Locke

After years of successful quail and hedgehog rearing, the belittling and insulting comments of friends finally took their toll. It was time for Mary to find a new career. After her short stint as DJ Piss and Moan pleased little and made even fewer dance— and the cancellation of Law & Order freed up her time—Mary decided to turn her spite outward. She now spends her late afternoons and evenings "researching" local bars not worth frequenting for Skint Press.

Thanks to...

Rachel Katz for honing my craft, Iowa for my perspective and to those for whom I am namesake—I say thank you.

the writers

introduction

PORTLAND   GEOGRAPHY

Before it flows into the Pacific Ocean, the Willamette River mingles with the waters of the Columbia River, between Washington and Oregon. The greater metro area is in the Willamette Valley, located between the Coastal and Cascade mountain range. The city of Portland is separated into five quadrants. The Willamette River separates the East from the West. Burnside Street separates the North from the South. North Williams Avenue separates the North from the Northeast side of Portland. (JB)

NEIGHBORHOODS

While most city lifelines are directed to the heart (read: downtown), Portland's pulse remains unique, instead traveling to the extremities (read: Portland's myriad of eclectic neighborhoods). As a result, visitors who stay downtown may get the impression that Portland does not have a thriving nightlife, when in reality, its vitality lies elsewhere. Portland is truly a collection of many small towns: neighborhoods with their own thriving strips, where the young flock to booze in hopes of a good time. Moreover, each neighborhood provides a distinctive atmosphere. The following summaries aim to be of use when you decide where to sleep, shop and spend your time. (ML)

ALBERTA STREET
Map Page 95

Ten years ago, you would not be able to walk down Alberta Street due to the gang violence and crack cocaine, but now you don't want to walk down the street, due to the whitewash of gentrification. From celebrated restaurants that cater meals to vegan canines, to toddler designer boutiques that make children the perfect accessory, little remains of the Alberta Street that once was (albeit Earl's Barber Shop). Alberta is another Portland hub: a street lined with heavy foot traffic, bars, clothing boutiques, and coffee shops. (ML)

 **Recommendations**

The Nest, The Know, Umpqua Bank

82ND AVENUE
Map Page 96

82nd Avenue, so dubbed for providing 82% of Portland's prostitution trade, offers many of the comforts of back home. On this street, you'll find the rampant racism of Mississippi, the two-story Pizza Hut/Taco Bell skyscrapers of Iowa, and enough meth to keep you as high as the cab drivers of New York City. This twenty-four hour farmers market of sleaze will leave you higher than a dime bag and lower than a belt buckle. (Casey Harris)

 **Recommendations**

Don't go here at night, or during the day.

HAWTHORNE/BELMONT
Map Page 96

In 1862 the long urban stretch that is now Southeast Hawthorne Boulevard was then known as Asylum Avenue, named after the Oregon State Hospital for the Insane Asylum that was once located there. Later in 1888, the street was renamed to honor

introduction

Dr. James C. Hawthorne, who was co-founder of the hospital—the name change came out of neighborhood residents' complaint that "Asylum Avenue" lacked tact. Today Hawthorne is lined with eclectic, arbitrary shops tailored to serve the hippies turned yuppies turned parents who stroll its sidewalks. (ML)

Recommendations

Mt. Tabor Park, Tabor Hill Cafe

HOLLYWOOD
Map Page 95

Make no mistake: there are no palm trees, celebrities or dreams of stardom in the Hollywood district. There are, however, a variety of markets, theaters, and independent shops located along Northeast Sandy Boulevard. These businesses cater to the residential neighborhood surrounding the Hollywood district, though not necessarily in a pedestrian-friendly fashion. When visiting the Hollywood district, it's best to have a particular destination and then venture out from there. (ML)

Recommendations

Sam's Hollywood Billiards

NORTH PORTLAND
Map Page 94

Once home to a large African American community, North Portland is now predominantly white. An influx of young property investors has pushed the bulk of the old North Portland neighborhood out. What remains is a hodgepodge of dive bars, corner shops, house shows and gentrified streets like Mississippi—a stomping ground for cheerful twenty-something's clutching lattes. (ML)

Recommendations

Maui's, Corner Spot, The Bluffs

OLD TOWN CHINATOWN
Map Page 93

Formerly a skid road, Old Town was revitalized in the 1970s, though no one told the countless transients who currently inhabit the area. The money and energy that was spent to repair and beautify Old Town creates a stark contrast against the homeless Portlanders who line the streets of Old Town and Chinatown with their shopping carts in tow. By day, Chinatown offers galleries and restaurants; by night, crack cocaine becomes the go-to medium of entertainment. (ML)

 **Recommendations**

Butters Gallery, Ground Kontrol

PEARL DISTRICT
Map Page 47

Formerly a derelict Northwest Industrial district, the Pearl District is now home to expensive salons, expensive bottle shops, expensive food fusion restaurants, expensive blah, blah, blah. If you're reading this book, you probably don't understand therapy for your dog, fifteen-dollar reverse osmosis coffee, or sustainable bamboo flooring. Put more simply: you just can't afford this area. The only reason to go to the Pearl is to have your white privilege reflected back at you. (ML)

 **Recommendations**

Low Brow Lounge, First Thursday

introduction

introduction

ST. JOHNS

Map Page 97

Incorporated into Portland in 1915, St. Johns still retains that isolated small town feel. It's home to the beautiful St. Johns Bridge, which was erected in 1931. Its Gothic cathedral style bridge-towers inspired the name of the equally lovely Cathedral Park, located just below it. When Portland seems too weird, take a cruise on Trimet Bus number 4 or 44 to spend a few hours in the bastion of blue collar that is St. Johns. (ML)

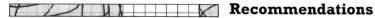 **Recommendations**

Slim's, St. John's Twin Cinema (matinee shows only), Cathedral Park

useful phrases

"Can I get some service, please?" Necessary to get the bartender to acknowledge you.

"I absolutely don't have any change/cigarettes." The lie you give to transients.

"He's just doing his thing." You have no idea why he braided his beard either.

"No worries." It's okay that you messed up my coffee order, ran over my foot, and/or insulted my mother.

"What do you mean I'm cut off?" Common last words given to Portland bartenders. (JB)

LANGUAGE

Portland vernacular is fairly straightforward. Locals take great pride in pronouncing Willamette as "will-am-it" (hint: it rhymes with "dammit"), Couch as "cooch," Glisan as "gleeson," and trucker speed as "pure cocaine." Portlanders may also refer to any visible mountain as "the mountain," and any river as "the river," though this ostensibly means Mount Hood and the Willamette, respectively. (JB)

LOCAL DRESS

The dress code of hipsters in the Pacific Northwest is distinct. Portland does not house the bleach blondes of Los Angeles, nor does it home the snow bunnies of Vancouver, British Columbia. To describe the fashion of men, one must start from the top and work down: the hair is unruly, scruffy at best. Facial hair suffers from a general lack of maintenance; beards and mustaches are prevalent, even among those whom they do not flatter. The more bushy and eccentric a beard, the better. The torso is preferably adorned with flannel for the colder days, and an ironic t-shirt for the warmer ones—the more ripped at the seams, the better. Wear and tear is a testament to its owner's apathy. In the two months of summer, men's thighs are painted with cut-off jean shorts of questionable above-the-knee-length, tight-rolled to secure position. During Portland's ten months of rainy, cold weather, skinny jeans are prevalent. Androgyny is a serious affliction.

introduction

For women, a similar conundrum exists. The look is decidedly relaxed. Hair maintains its natural mousey brown luster or is dyed a bright pink to establish the inner weirdo for those ladies over 30. The makeup is remarkably absent and is representative of the plain, no-worries-girl who lies beneath. Brow waxing is not essential—nor is mustache waxing. For the torso, subdued colors of browns, hunter greens and grays are most popular, notably in the shape of a cardigan or v-neck. Moving south, gray or brown knee-length skirts covering black or gray leggings are undeniably popular. Knee-length socks complete the layered ensemble. These knee-length socks are always a different shade of bland that does not clash with the skirt or leggings. On her feet are knee-high boots, which almost entirely conceal the aforementioned knee-length socks, rendering them inconsequential. These knee-high boots vary from cowboy to rain boots. Also common: just tights—no pants (this is met with little qualm from their male counterparts). As one Portlander remarked, "It adds a little sunshine to the dreary days."

For accessories, the fixed gear bicycle, messenger bag and hoodie are popular among both sexes. (ML)

SPORTS

Portland is home to a variety of professional sports teams (the Timbers of soccer, the Winterhawks of hockey) with varying degrees of popularity—the front-runners being the often-disappointing NBA Portland Trailblazers. Longtime fans blame the coaching, though they will accept the following explanations with deliberation: bad trades, bad "D," bad year, bad hustle, bad hometown advantage, and Oden being injured. When they're at the Rose Garden Arena, Blazers games are one of the largest draws in the NBA, contributing to the phenomenon known as "Blazermania."

The second most popular past time in the city is choosing sides in the football rivalry between the University of Oregon Ducks and the Oregon State University Beavers. Though neither team is located in Portland, the "Civil War" game is the largest football event in the city. In the mid 2000s, portions of the under-thirty population attempted ironic popular sports fan participation, rooting for the Blazers with sarcastic fanaticism (probably because of the availability of vintage sports clothing), but in recent years there has been an upswing in Blazers attendance and Beavers/Ducks side-taking. No one has ever attempted an ironic following of the Timbers.

There exists in Portland a great number of adult sports leagues that operate with various levels of formality. As the seriousness of the activity increases, popularity and participation decrease. This being so, the city is a cycle-polo and kickball powerhouse, but weak when it comes to non-lesbian baseball teams. It must be noted that there are sports for which this is not true: roller-derby and cycling are very popular and are enjoyed by a number of humorless practitioners. (JB)

introduction

CHAPTER 2

BOOZE

Portland culture is deeply rooted in drinking. It has more bars per capita than most cities in the U.S. But not all bars are created equal. Some are chic, high-brow establishments for the folks who save their entire paycheck for just one weekend. Other drinkers with lower standards need their nectar through-out the week, and must satisfy this craving on a budget. This sliver of society prefers Hamm's to Rolling Rock and Whiskey Beer Backs to Lavender-infused Lemon Drops. These patrons don't want to spread their wallets as thin as their livers. Therefore, Skint has detailed the cheapest methods for inebriation. From the low-down on corner shops, to a thorough list of liquor stores, to top picks for dives, Skint has your libations covered. (ML)

corner stores

If your excessive Whiskey Beer Backs are getting too expensive, it might be best to embrace the recession and stay in. When the "But-I-must-do-my-part-to-support-the-economy" line no longer rationalizes every night out, it's time to drink in your living room, a hotel lobby or a backyard. In which case, you'll find the best deals for cheap beer not found in chain stores like the Plaid or Seven Eleven, but at the Mom and Pop stores on the corner. The best locations appear in North Portland. Here, corner shops are often across the street and kitty corner from one another, where an over-supply of twenty-four ounce malt liquor drives down market price. Seek these places out first, but head to the chain stores for your take-away nightcap, as the corner shops typically close by midnight. (ML)

liquor stores

Oregon ranks only slightly better than Minnesota in its embrace of prohibitive Puritan values. In the state of Oregon, you can't buy liquor at grocery stores and gas stations. In this state, there's no rolling into your local Hy-Vee at a quarter to two in the morning with the assurance that your next day will be ruined by a hangover and regret. No—here, you can only purchase your booze from liquor stores run by the Oregon Liquor Control Commission. Each location has its own specific hours, but none are open later than ten in the evening, and few are open on Sundays. In Portland, you must plan ahead for that gin on your hip. (ML)

DOWNTOWN

550 SW Washington St.
Mon-Sat 10:30am-6pm,
Sun 12pm-5pm
503.227.2791

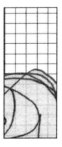

925 SW 10th Ave.
Mon-Sat 11am-7pm
503.227.3391

2075 SW First Ave., Suite 1B
Mon-Thurs 10am-7pm,
Fri-Sat 10am-8pm,
Sun 12pm-6pm
503.241.9354

1 NW 23rd Pl.
Mon-Sat 10am-7pm
503.227.0338

900 NW Lovejoy St., Suite 140
Mon-Fri 9am-10pm,
Sat 10am-10pm,
Sun 12pm-7pm
503.477.8604

SOUTHWEST

550 SW Washington St.
Mon-Sat 10:30am-6pm,
Sun 12pm-5pm
503.227.2791

925 SW 10th Ave.
Mon-Sat 11am-7pm
503.227.3391

2075 SW First Ave., Suite 1B
Mon-Thurs 10am-7pm,
Fri-Sat 10am-8pm,
Sun 12pm-6pm
503.241.9354

SOUTHEAST

1040 SE Hawthorne Blvd.
Mon-Sat 10am-7pm,
Sun 11am-5pm
503.236.2076

4638 SE Hawthorne Blvd.
Mon-Thurs 10am-7pm,
Fri-Sat 10am-8pm
503.235.1573

7207 SE Milwaukie Ave.
Mon-Sat 10am-8pm
503.235.3635

5120 SE Powell Blvd.
Mon-Thurs 10am-8pm,
Fri-Sat 10am-9pm
503.771.8107

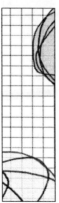

4324 SE Woodstock Blvd.
Mon-Sat 10am-7pm,
Sun 12pm-5pm
503.777.3058

NORTHEAST

3334 NE Killingsworth St.
Mon-Thurs 11am-7pm,
Fri-Sat 11am-8pm
503.282.0178

3738 NE Sandy Blvd.
Mon-Thurs 11am-7pm,
Fri-Sat 11am-10pm,
Sun 12pm-5pm
503.284.0987

3532 NE MLK Jr. Blvd.
Mon-Sat 11am-7pm
503.493.3473

1621 NE 9th Ave.
Mon-Sat 11am-8pm,
Sun 1pm-6pm
503.288.0961

7253 NE Sandy Blvd.
Mon-Sat 9:30am-9pm,
Sun 11am-4pm
503.284.7591

NORTH

8221 N Denver Ave.
Mon-Sat 11am-7pm
503.285.1776

8915 N Lombard St.
Mon-Sat 10am-7pm
503.286.3931

dives

Corner stores offer the most economical version of intoxication. The Oregon Liquor Control Commission's monopoly of liquor stores delivers the cheapest price per ounce of Monopolowa Vodka, Jim Beam Bourbon or anything by the Monarch label (for when the destination is more important than the journey). But what you don't get from the Mike's Harder Lemonade from the reach-in cooler or the pulls from the bottle in your living room, is the expectation of the unexpected that a night out on the town provides. When one more party after eleven o'clock is going to get you thrown out of your hostel, or when the front desk clerk of the Viking Motel becomes increasingly suspicious of your mood-altering "apple juice," it's time to venture out. Skint recommends the following bars, because this foray into the night need not be expensive, or pretentious. (ML)

DOWNTOWN

Kelly's Olympian
426 SW Washington St. 503.228.3669
Open daily 10am-2:30am
        Bus #8
Kelly's is Portland's third oldest bar, which opened in 1902 with Olympia beer as its specialty. These days, the owners employ an elaborate motorcycle/racing theme, which explains the dozen actual hogs dangling precariously overhead as you drink. It's an oasis amidst the douchery of downtown, where cheap breakfast is served all day and the bar's full menu is available until close—rare for downtown or anywhere. Late night food specials kick in at midnight during the week. (MB)

Red Cap Garage
1025 SW Stark St. 503.226.4171
Sun-Mon 4pm-12am, Tues-Sat 4pm-2am
        Bus #20 Portland Streetcar
Go to the Red Cap Garage early for a laid back atmosphere and $2.50 well drinks, or head in late when things get a little more raucous for

dives

$2.50 well drinks. This gay bar, located across from the Ace Hotel, pours the cheap booze during every open hour. (ML)

Scooter McQuade's

1321 SW Washington St. 503.248.4060
Open daily 10am-2am
  Bus #20

Sip your whiskey at Scooter's, one of the rare downtown bars where you can forget you're in downtown Portland: the service is friendly, the drinks aren't exorbitant and no one is dressed like he's in a band. I'm scared to give this bar up, but more people need to have a night they'll have trouble remembering here. (ML)

The Yamhill Pub

223 SW Yamhill St. 503.295.6613
Open daily 10am-2am
  Max Red/Blue, Yamhill District Max Station

The Yamhill Pub is a study in poor life decisions, and unless you've made a few, you aren't gonna like this place. That said, even if you've never set foot inside, it deserves respect for being the shittiest, grossest, and last bar standing in the cleaned-up facade that is downtown. The drinks are cheap and strong, the food inedible, the clientele depressing, and the bathrooms are, well, derelict. Like you, the Yamhill has never gotten any breaks and it shows. But, goddammit, Portland, I love the place. (JB)

NORTH

Farmer's Barn

7421 N Denver Ave. 503.283.3044
Open daily 7am-2:30am   Cash only
  Bus #4

Unmistakably red and barn-like, this place, has the strangest layout. There's the main bar, made of beautiful quartz stone, and then random bars throughout the cavernous building, including one in the shape of a cross. Populating the space daily and nightly are true salt-of-the-earth folks who will not hesitate to chat you up about sports, or high school memories. To avoid them, play free pool, Video Poker, or eat amazingly cheap bar food. (MB)

Kenton Club

2025 N Kilpatrick St. 503.285.3718
Open daily 10am-2:30am
　　　　Bus #4, Max Yellow, Kenton Station
The World Famous Kenton Club (so dubbed because of its appearance in the illustrious '70s roller derby film "Kansas City Bomber") is located in North Portland's Kenton district. Its locale is "so hot right now" but the Kenton Club proprietors either don't know or don't care. The bar maintains a divey atmosphere as tacky as its rock-wall exterior. Pound dirt-cheap drinks over a game of pool, on the large back patio, or inside, while you watch the free show. Know that if you're female and choose to dance, a certain old timer who frequents the place might approach you and ask for a spin. You can say no, but say yes to have the full Kenton club experience. (MB)

Maui's

3508 N Williams Ave. 503.282.1611
Mon-Sat 3pm-2:30am, Sun 9:30am-2:30am
　　　　Bus #4, 24, 44
Maui's serves as the compromise between dive bar and hip bar: the whiskey pours stiff, but the atmosphere isn't ho-hum, after-work quiet. This place is the go-to tropical oasis in North Portland when you're not in the mood for Vendetta, the Crow Bar, or the Florida Room. (ML)

Slim's Restaurant and Lounge

8635 N Lombard St. 503.286.3854
Open daily 7am-2:30am
　　　　Bus #4, 75
In local history, this place (est. 1911) originated the term "dive," but new owners have made Slim's a dive with a funky sheen. It's now a nucleus for a robust crowd of aging hippies, young

dives

wannabe-bohemians, and light-hearted thugs who faithfully pack the place during weekly events like Monday Bingo and Tuesday Open Mic. Occasional live music ranges from reggae to Irish. And this may be your only chance to try "Tachos,"—tots and nachos combined in one glorious dish. (MB)

Yorgo's

5421 N Greeley Ave. 503.283.0676
Mon-Thurs 11:30am-12am,
Fri-Sat 11:30am-2:30am, Sun 9am-12am
Bus #72

After many years as a delightfully decrepit hole-in-the-wall, Yorgo's has recently become part of the North Portland renaissance that turns corner bars into the type of place your average yuppie will enjoy. In addition to big screen TVs and Video Lottery, there's now a poker table, shuffleboard, and a horribly obnoxious digital jukebox. It is still a place of interest, given its location (last stop on Killingsworth). Yorgo's also offers a daily-rotating menu of cheap food and drink specials, and the interesting mix of new and old clientele. Also, free computer access with internet. (MB)

what was once

What's left of Joe's Place—the blue collar bastion that served old Alberta's black community before gentrification—is a large, obscured sign that hangs above the pool table at The Nest. It acts as an homage and reminder of the bar and the tight-knit community that once resided there. (ML)

NORTHEAST

The B-Side

632 E Burnside St. 503.233.3113
Open daily 4pm-2:30am
Bus #6, 12, 19, 20

The B-side is one of those arty dives that can sidetrack you before you stroll over the bridge to downtown. The crowd is, by Portland standards, pleasantly

dives

unpretentious—you'll never find yourself wondering what the fuck you're doing here, unlike when you're sitting in a booth at the Doug Fir. (JB)

Billy Ray's Neighborhood Dive

2216 NE MLK Jr. Blvd. 503.287.7254

Open daily 12pm-2:30am   Cash Only
         Bus #6

Billy Ray's emerges out of the desolate stretch of urban thoroughfare that is MLK Blvd. Located in a red, two-story house, this dive offers all the comforts of home without the family or chores. Enjoy chilled twenty-two-ounce mugs of beer and Swanson microwave dinners at the cozy bar while you watch cable TV shows alongside super friendly barkeeps. Or, just put some quarters into one of the finest jukeboxes in town and cram into one of the extremely narrow booths. There's also the back patio (most glorious in summer—don't miss the BBQs) and the rickety, living room inspired top floor, decked out with couches, pool and pinball. Skip the men's restroom, with no locking stall or toilet seat and head towards the ladies' room: there's never a line. (MB)

The Know

2026 NE Alberta St. 503.473.8729

Mon-Fri 4pm-2am, Sat-Sun 3pm-2am
         Bus #72

The Know boasts a smoking alley, a pool table, disgusting bathrooms with no locks, and karaoke on Sundays. The bands that play here are very loud, and the people who watch them ride trains, and dress in black with patches and leather. The drinks are formidable, but there's always a beer for a few bucks. In a neighborhood swarming with shitty hippies driving whatever the modern-day-Mazda-Miata is, this bar is real okay. (CR)

dives

The Nest

1801 NE Alberta St. 503.282.0230
Open daily 3pm-2am
      Bus # 72

At first glance, The Nest is just another painstakingly dived bar for the painstakingly poor rich kids that live in and frequent the Alberta neighborhood. However, this shining paradigm of gentrification is worth the trip. People who know how to play pool, play pool here. The jukebox at this bar is hemorrhaging with music that drunks love, and during the summer the huge back patio is swarming with crusty bike hippies playing ping-pong and horseshoes. There's a full menu of good food, and I'll bet you didn't know that all the bartenders here get benefits. Take that, The Man. (CR)

NORTHWEST

Low Brow Lounge

1036 NW Hoyt St. 503.226.0200
Mon-Sat 3pm-2:30am, Sun 6pm-12am $10 card min
      Bus #17, Portland Streetcar

The attendants at the Froelick, Anka and Butters galleries (Art Gallery map page 47) know that you're not in the market for that fifteen-hundred-dollar geometric two-tone painting of koi—not that they couldn't tell the second you walked in the door, anyway. So now, stop into the dimly lit Low Brow Lounge: the only dive bar in the Pearl. Their happy hour starts up conveniently after the galleries close down. Fuel up on a few Pabsts here then head up to Scooter McQuade's (page 22). (ML)

Tony's Tavern

1955 W Burnside St. 503.228.4574
Open daily 8am-2:30am   Cash only
      Bus #20

Past the mirrored booths, the wood paneling, and the post-cougar ladies at the bar, you'll find the Miller tap on display in Tony's Tavern. This tap pours two-dollar mini pitchers from eight in the morning until seven-thirty in the evening. Catch a buzz here before heading out to a livelier bar. (ML)

SOUTHEAST

dives

Basement Pub

1028 SE 12th Ave. 503.231.6068

Mon-Fri 3pm-2am, Sat-Sun 12pm-2am

Bus #15, 70

On the higher end of cheap, the Basement Pub offers good, inexpensive pub food all night long. The back patio is inviting and the tables are free of graffiti—which is either a reflection of a recent refurbishment or the maturity of the clientele. The patio's proximity to the surrounding residential neighbors ensures a quiet night, so get fed and fueled here and head somewhere dingier afterward. (ML)

Gil's Speakeasy

609 ½ SE Taylor St. 503.234.8991

Sun-Thurs 12pm-Late Fri-Sat 12pm-2:30am

Bus #6, 10, 14, 15

Drink where the sun don't shine at the divy-ist of dive bars—Gil's Speakeasy. No patio, no booths, Gil's has just hard wooden tables and chairs, a few shitty couches, un-shit-able bathrooms, and Keno. Order the whiskey-beer-back and end your night here. You can compare your drunken ceiling signature to the one from the last time you don't remember being at Gil's. (ML)

My Father's Place

523 SE Grand Ave. 503.235.5494

Open daily 6am–2:30am

Bus #6

After roughly 30 years (still boasting original wait staff! Zing!) of not particularly good food and not especially cheap drinks, My Father's Place inexplicably remains a Portland institution. The filthy, dimly lit cavern is the default choice of the hungover looking for chicken fried steak and mimosas (prepared and served in any range from "well and prompt" to "palatable and ineptly"). The prices have been climbing steadily in the past few years, but Portlanders' affinity for this unremarkable restaurant/bar ensure that MFP will be around indefinitely. (JB)

dives

'Reel M' Inn [sic]
2430 SE Division St. 503.231.3880
Mon-Sat 10am-2:30am, Sun 10am–1am
Bus #4

'Reel M' Inn is not only a fantastic dive,—they've also got the best fried chicken in Southeast, and the bartenders won't look at you funny for getting extra Jo-Jo's. (IF)

Space Room
4800 SE Hawthorne Blvd. 503.235.8303
Mon-Fri 11am-2am, Sat-Sun 8am-2am
Bus #4, 14

The Space Room is a dark hole-in-the-wall on the eastern end of Hawthorne. It's one of those places where you might find a questionable bag of white powder on the bathroom floor. The entrees and appetizers aren't cheap, but the Jim Beam is only four dollars, so if that doesn't keep you coming back, the sparkly interior décor will. (IF)

The Vern
2622 SE Belmont St. 503.233.7851
Open daily 1pm-2:30am
Bus #15

Technically, its name is Hanigan's, but no one calls it that. The Vern's loving nickname comes from the destruction of this bar's ubiquitous TAVERN sign, which left it with only its last four letters intact. By day, it's a great spot to watch Soaps and re-runs with guys who have ponytails and a bartender who claims she'll be there until she "dies or gets old." By night, it's home to the studded, leather-clad and dyed-black-hair crowd, who are wooed by cheap beer, a stacked jukebox, pool, foosball and video poker. (MB)

CHAPTER 3

VIA

Getting into Portland, getting around, and getting away from Portland all cost money. But with this guide, transportation will not bankrupt your trip. Once you find an affordable method of arrival, you'll be able to get around with meager means. Skint provides the tools to avoid that regrettable cab ride back to the hostel you chose because you didn't know any better. Skint spares you these dollars by providing details on bicycle and public transportation options, as well as progressive car rental alternatives. (MB, ML)

an alternative to airport prices Ikea

Mon-Sun 9:30am – 8 pm;
Breakfast until 11am

If you're traveling in or out of PDX, it's well worth it to skip the airport restaurants and get on the Red line to nearby Cascade Station. Get off at the first stop (Cascade Station) and you'll arrive at Ikea. Go up the main stairs and find the Scandinavian cafeteria, lined with open faced shrimp and egg sandwiches, meat or vegetable wraps, mini salad bar, and hot foods, including meatballs and a variety of pastas. Avoid the Alfredo sauce at all costs. The coffee is palatable and only a buck, with free refills. Dart and weave through the entire store to get to the ground floor exit, where you'll find the dollar hot dogs and ice cream. The Ikea restaurant experience is only recommended for light packers. (ML)

arrive

Transportation into Portland can be quite costly, but ways to minimize these expenses do exist. From being flexible in travel dates to holding certain advantage cards, there are ways you can make it to Portland on a reasonable budget. (MB)

BUS

Greyhound Bus Terminal
greyhound.com
550 NW 6th Ave. 503.243.2361
Open daily 5:45am-11:00pm
   Bus #4, 8, 9, 17, 33, 35, 44
   Max Green/Yellow, Union Station

Catch a ride with dirty Juggalos and terrorists who can't afford plane tickets on the Dirty Dog. It's cheaper to book your bus tickets really far in advance online. Greyhound gives discounts to active military personnel, veterans and students, but students have to buy the Student Advantage card in advance. (ML)

AIR

Flying into Portland
While there is no cheap way to fly domestically in the States (where's our Ryanair?), some cheap online travel agents do exist—namely, cheapoair.com, kayak.com and expedia.com. When choosing dates, Tuesday through Thursday are the least expensive

on which to fly. If you're a student, use that to your advantage and visit studentuniverse.com. Create an account with your university email address and save some money (but not much). Another option for students is statravel.com, the travel site that started ISIC—the International Student Identification Card. It offers a number of okay discounts. If flying is too expensive (and it often is), check out Ridesharing.

After arriving in Portland, if you do choose to fly in, bypass the rental car stations at the airport. Don't even step outside to hail a cab. The Max Red Line will pick you up at the airport and get you where you need to go. After picking up your luggage, follow the signs to the Max. Go to the ticket machines—and this is important: before inserting your money, select your ticket type first (a two hour, all zone pass is optimal). You can also visit the Trimet website (trimet.org) in advance to plan your trip from the airport to motel/hostel/friend's place. (ML)

TRAIN

Amtrak Union Station

amtrak.com

800 NW 6th Ave. Open daily 7:15am-9:15pm

Bus #9, 33, 77, Max Yellow/Green, Union Station

While not the least expensive way to travel up and down the coast and through the Cascades, it is certainly the most romantic. Small discounts are available for ISIC and Student Advantage cardholders. (ML)

around

Even stronger than Portland's reputation as a haven for hipsters and brewpubs is its reputation as a bicycle-friendly city. A plethora of streets are painted with the white diamond lane that is devoted to cycling commuters. A multitude of shops rent out bikes at reasonable rates. For those who still believe bicycles are only to be ridden on the sidewalk and around the block, Portland's public transportation system, Trimet, was recently voted one of the best in the country for its consistent and expansive service. (MB, ML)

BICYCLE

You can't go back to the Midwest after visiting Portland without skimming through books at Powell's, eating cheap steak at the Acropolis or riding a bicycle—in the street, that is. Depending on how long you stay in Portland, you may be able to flip a bike off of Craigslist (portland.craigslist. org/bik/). It takes some initial capital for the investment, but if you can afford it, you may be able to make some money, break even or own your own bike. If you don't think you'll be able to flip it in time, rent one. Of the bike shops listed below, all have pretty similar pricing. However, depending on what kind of bike you need (urban or off-road) and for how long, you can get a slightly better deal if you know what you want. Portland Tour Bicycles (345 NW Everett St., 503.360.6815, www.portlandbicycletours.com/rentals.html) offers great hourly, daily and weekly deals on cruisers and street bikes, ensuring you'll be able to go from bar to bar and then to the show quicker than a bus and cheaper than a cab. Clever Cycles (908 SE Hawthorne Blvd., 503.334.1560, clevercycles.com/services/rentals/) provides cheap rates for hourly and daily rates, and even throws in all the bells and whistles, and helmets. Another good daily and weekly rate is offered by Pedal Bike Tours (2249 N Williams Ave., 503.877.2453, pedalbiketours.com/bike-rentals/index.shtml), their city bikes are multi-speed and they don't offer hourly rates. The only deal offered by Waterfront Bicycles (10 SW Ash St. #100, 503.227.1719, www.waterfrontbikes.com/rentals) is their weekly rate on hybrids; otherwise, stick with the other guys. (ML)

around

CAR

Zipcar
zipcar.com

Zipcars are in abundance in the Portland metro area. It's more advantageous if you already have an account, as setting it up can take a few weeks. Once you have your Zipcard, you can reserve the cars online, by the hour, with gas and insurance included. You can drive for up to 180 miles without racking up any fees, making it a novel choice for day trips to Mt. Hood or the Gorge. Businesses get special hourly rates, so legitimize your little record label and reap the benefit. (ML)

TRANSIT

Trimet
trimet.org

If you don't have a car, a bicycle or a friend's bicycle, you'll soon become acquainted with Portland's mass transit system, Trimet. The buses, trains, and streetcar of Trimet provide a pretty frequent, fairly reliable, and far-reaching public transport service. You can call Trimet at 503.238.RIDE or visit the website (trimet.org) to plan the buzzed trip from the Acropolis to the tacos at Santa Cruz in St. Johns. (ML)

Bus

As the bus approaches, read the display at the top to make sure you're boarding the correct bus. When you board a Portland bus, you'll greet the driver and put your two dollars and a nickel into the machine. Neither the machine nor the driver will give change. The driver will hand you a transfer that's good for at least two hours. Hold onto this. It's good on the Max and the Streetcar as well. If you're not sure of your stop, ask the bus driver. Bus drivers can be surprisingly pleasant considering the monotony and rudeness they regularly endure. When you're coming up to your stop, pull one of the yellow cords. Try to exit out of the back of the bus, even though few actually do this. Don't forget to thank your driver upon departure. (ML)

around

Max

Stealing a ride on the train is notoriously easy in Portland. Board the Max and hope security doesn't get on at a later stop. Ticket checkers used to wear bright yellow jackets making them very easy to dodge. But now they're getting smarter by dressing undercover. They can stop you on the train, as you're getting off the train, and as you're leaving any Max stop. If you choose the good Samaritan/not an asshole route, you can buy a ticket before you board: there are automated ticket machines located on most platforms. To buy a ticket, first pick your ticket type (two hour, all day, etc.) and follow the screen directions from there—don't insert your money first. You can purchase weekly and monthly passes at these machines as well. Unfortunately, the machines are consistently fussy. Often they're broken ("Out of Service"), or won't accept cash. In these instances you have to run to the next stop (infuriating) or find another platform (stupid) or pay with your card (annoying). And ticket inspectors will still expect you to have a ticket even if you've encountered a broken machine. You may be able to get away with a warning, but they can issue a citation and a fine of $115.

Board the Red, Blue, Yellow and Green lines downtown—where they are free up until the Rose Quarter—and travel throughout Portland to the different suburbs. The Blue going East takes you to Gresham; going West, it takes you to Beaverton, and then to Hillsboro. The Green will take you to Clackamas Town Center. You don't want to go to any of these places. The Yellow, however, heading North to the Expo Center will take you to North Portland and the horse track (Portland Meadows page 49). The Red can take you to the airport. Each transit stop has a map and pay phone to help you along the way. (ML)

Streetcar

The Streetcar will take you from the Waterfront to Slabtown (page 65), but you can walk to your destination faster than the streetcar can get you there. So unless it's raining, just walk. (ML)

away

After soaking up the urban landscape of Portland, do not pass up the inexpensive opportunities to enjoy the Oregon riches that lie just beyond. (MB)

Rideshare

erideshare.com | portland.craigslist.org/rid/

Splitting gas money is typically cheaper than bus fare, but with rideshare there's always the gamble of getting smashed into the back of a sedan with some jerks. That aside, the biggest challenge is finding the right route at the right time. The travel section of erideshare.com is helpful, as is the rideshare section of Portland's Craigslist (portland.craigslist.org/rid/), which is full of rides up and down the coast and beyond. (ML)

Northwest Point

northwest-point.com

541.484.4100 for questions

Office hours Mon-Fri 8am-5pm

Northwest Point is a coach service with routes from Portland to Oregon's Northern coastal cities (from Cannon Beach to Astoria). Check their website for route details. It's only an hour and a half by coach—a modern coach equipped with Wi-Fi and power outlets—to the Pacific Ocean. Tickets can be purchased in person at the Portland Greyhound or Amtrak stations, or online through the Amtrak website (tickets.amtrak.com). If you carry an ISIC or Student Advantage card, it'll get you a discount. (ML)

CHAPTER 4

SLEEP

The most expensive part of traveling is finding an afford-able place to rest your head at night. The following recommenda-tions are the least expensive places to crash in Portland, and they cover every comfort level—from an outside sleepover at Wash-ington Park to a warm, safe bunk in a hostel, to a seedier (though more thrilling) stopover such as the Joyce Hotel. The prices for the following recommended accommodations never amount to more than forty-five dollars a night (the Viking Motel)—that is, before the Oregon state lodger's tax of 12.5%. (ML)

Airbnb

airbnb.com

When couch surfing seems too sketchy, look into airbnb, a website where folks rent out rooms in their homes, by the night. The site often provides information about the rental room's location in Portland. However, their descriptions of the neighborhoods for the room listings can be a little misleading, as they are, after all, trying to sell you something. Therefore it's best to use Skint's guide to Portland neighborhoods to get an idea of which neighborhood is best suited for you. (ML)

Couchsurfing

couchsurfing.org

Couchsurfing.org has over three hundred couches up for crashing. Browse through the profiles to find an unpretentious host who is accepting of your drinking problem. Stay for free, but please, do the dishes. (ML)

DOWNTOWN

Joyce Hotel

322 SW 11th Ave. 503.243.6757

Bus #20 Portland Streetcar

Channel your inner Bukowski while smoking rollies in your very own walk-in closet with a bed. Listen to the subtle sounds of domestic violence through Joyce's paper thin walls, while you write, "Need spare change" in Sharpie on a piece of cardboard for tomorrow's shift at work. Joyce Hotel is for the wild at heart—not the faint of heart—but its rates are affordable and it's centrally located. It fills up fast at the beginning of the month, so book accordingly. (ML)

Recommendations

Enough cannot be said of the inebriated good times that come out of the downtown hole-in-the-wall **Scooter McQuade's** (page 22). Their specials change often, but they remain consistent bargains. The $2.50 price for well drinks offered by the **Red Cap Garage** (page 21) is incredible for a downtown bar. (ML)

sleep

sleep

Likewise, the **Yamhill Pub** (page 22) is worth the short trek from the Joyce. The cheapest way to get fed is the **food cart pod** at SW 10th Avenue and SW Washington Street. If you're in the mood to visit a city of books, check out **Powell's** (page 82) and then head down Couch Street to mash some buttons on The Simpsons arcade game at **Ground Kontrol** (page 44). (ML)

Kent Hotel
308 SW 12th Ave. 503.243.6757
> Bus #20, Portland Streetcar

An extension of the Joyce Hotel; contact them for booking. (ML)

NORTH

Friendly Bike Guest House
friendlybikeguesthouse.com
4039 N Williams Ave. 503.799.2615
> Bus #44

Geared towards cyclists, but open to everyone, the Friendly Bike Guesthouse offers the best deal for accommodation in North and Northeast Portland. FBG is (slightly) more expensive than the hostels in the Southeast and Northwest, but this downside is offset by the bountiful cheaper restaurants, dives, and house shows nearby. At FBG, you can put in a load of laundry, repair your bike at the mechanic's stand, and surf the Google on their free WIFI to the hum of the dishwasher working away in the kitchen. There is a three-day minimum to stay, which is in place to foster a sense of community—a simple commitment, considering the modern and clean facilities. (ML)

Recommendations

For a proper booze-up when staying at the Friendly Bike Guesthouse, head over to **Maui's** (page 23). If you're looking for cheap eats, walk over to Mississippi Avenue and choose from one of the many **food carts** (go for Mexican over Asian fusion). Also, for inexpensive, quality produce, **Cherry Sprouts** (722 N Sumner St.) is unparalleled. Bus #4 will pick you up on Mississippi Street and drop you off right at Cherry Sprouts. The #44 will you pick you up out front and you can get close if you exit the bus at the Alberta stop. A closer option is the **Hostess Retail Outlet** (115 N Cook St.), which can supply all your day-old bread needs. If you want to spend some money on material items, be sure to hit up the **Record Room** (page 85), **Mississippi Records** (page 84), and **In Other Words Bookstore** (page 81). For free items, visit the freecycle known as the **Black Rose Collective** (page 79). If you're looking to drink free beer from tiny sample cups, schedule a tour at the **Widmer Brewery** (page 50), and afterward take the Max Yellow Line up North to the Prescott Station and enjoy the view from the **Bluffs** (page 48).

Viking Motel

6701 N Interstate Ave. 800.308.5097

Bus #44, Max Yellow, Rosa Parks Station

The Viking Motel resides up along Interstate Avenue, among the long stretch of temporary housing motels. Its neon lights may not shine the brightest, but its rates are the cheapest. One to two people can stay in a double room for forty-five dollars a night, provided they mention they found the special rate advertised on the Viking Motel website (i.e.—not this book). The Viking Motel is typical in that it boasts free HBO, a mini fridge and morning coffee. But the real charm lies in its location: on the MAX line in North Portland—meaning you stay in a cheap neighborhood, then take the train south to downtown, or north to the horse track (Portland Meadows page 49) to earn some extra spending money. (ML)

Recommendations

Close to the Viking Motel, **George's Corner Sports Bar** (5501 N Interstate Ave) and **Farmer's Barn** (page 22) both offer blue collar, hamburger-oriented, sports bar experiences. **Saratoga** (page 64) is for the younger, show-going crowd that prefers their hamburgers a little more fancy. Hamburgers aside, the **King Burrito** (page 71) is a well-lit, carpeted dining option, and the **Corner Spot Tavern** (page 67) offers the cheapest breakfast on this side of downtown. To freshen up your bric-a-brac collection, visit the **North Portland Goodwill** (3134 N Lombard St).

sleep

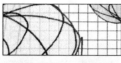

when the White Eagle was affordable

In the early twentieth century, long before the McMeniman brothers flipped the White Eagle as part of their franchise, the building was home to a different saloon owned by two Eastern European brothers. Their bar served mostly dock workers who worked in the area. They offered the now sorely missed free lunch option— a popular citywide practice, which was adopted in order to lure potential drinkers. During the prohibition, the White Eagle transitioned into a soft drink emporium, that was merely a front for a speakeasy. (ML)

For fun, take a dip in the pool at the **Peninsula Park Rose Garden** (700 N Rosa Parks Way) or go to **pc-pdx.com** to find a show in the area. (ML)

White Eagle Saloon

mcmenamins.com/whiteeagle
836 N Russell St. 503.282.6810
Bus #35, 85 Max Yellow, Albina/ Mississippi Station

Forty-five dollars gets you a private bunk, a sink in your room, and a shared bathroom down the hall. However, you'll have to contend with Indie-Alt-Country bands playing the bar downstairs and no decent dives for a mile. The only cheap food you'll find here— without trekking up the hill to some Mississippi Avenue carts—is the happy hour that still charges over two dollars for a pint of PBR. Good place to put your bags down, but you'll undoubtedly want to explore outside of the vicinity quickly. (ML)

Recommendations

If you're in need of some swill, skip the bar located beneath you and bus it to **Billy Ray's Dive Bar** (page 25). There the PBR flows into twenty-two ounce mugs instead of the typical sixteen. To avoid drinking on an empty stomach, grab a slice at **Sparky's Pizza** (2434 NE MLK Blvd.) before heading in. The next day browse through vinyl at **Mississippi Records** (page 84) in hopes that a little retail therapy will cure your hangover. The **Black Rose Collective** (page 79)—a freecycle located across the street from the record shop—is worth a visit. For fun, tour the **Widmer Brewery** (page 50) and get a free pint glass, or jump on the Max Yellow Line and head downtown. (ML)

NORTHWEST

HI Portland

nwportlandhostel.com
Northwest 425 NW 18th Ave. 503.241.2783
    Bus #17

HI Portland – Northwest offers the typical Hosteling International experience. This place has the standard clean bunk beds, free Wi-Fi, storage and maps—offered up in an expensive Northwest neighborhood. As always, add three dollars to any bunk price if you aren't a Hosteling International member (all the same, it's one of the cheapest, safest places to stay in Portland). (ML)

Recommendations

HI Portland is in a very intoxication-oriented location: a short jaunt over to Burnside and you're smack dab along a row of blue-collar dives. **Tony's Tavern** (page 26) is one such establishment, as is the **Marathon Taverna** (page 68)—both offer inexpensive, greasy breakfasts. **Eat Pizza!** (page 73) provides some lunch while you're in the area. To burn off the calories you've just consumed, jog through **Powell's ("City of") Books** (page 82), then head over to **Everyday Music** (page 83) and thumb through their discount records. For fun, take a stroll through nature's work of art: the **International Rose Test Garden** (page 54). (ML)

SOUTHEAST

Portland Hawthorne Hostel

portlandhostel.org
3031 SE Hawthorne Blvd. 503.236.3380   Non-members add $3
    Bus #14

Portland Hawthorne Hostel offers the least sketchy bed in town in the second most gentrified and annoying Portland neighborhood (the Pearl District is number one). Hawthorne offers an

sleep

abundance of white families dressed for urban hiking, walking up and down a street lined with over-priced coffee shops, record shops, boutiques and breakfast joints. The Portland Hawthorne Hostel appears to be in the thick of it all, but, in reality, you'll end up busing out of the neighborhood to get a cheap drink at a dive bar. This neighborhood will make you hate Portland. (ML)

Recommendations

The Hawthorne neighborhood offers little in the way of drinking. Best to jump on a bus and get the hell out of there. For groceries, go to the **Fred Meyer** (3805 SE Hawthorne Blvd.) and cook for yourself in the hostel kitchen to save some money. When you get sick of cheap tomato sauce served over enriched macaroni product, head over to the **Tabor Hill Café** (page 69). The prices on their menu are high, but their specials board deserves a once-over. For vinyl shopping, **Exiled** (page 83) or **Green Noise Records** (page 84) are top picks. If you're looking for a cheap night out on Hawthorne, your best bet is a movie at the **Bagdad Theater** (3702 SE Hawthorne Blvd). (ML)

SOUTHWEST

Washington Park
washingtonparkpdx.org
SW Portland 503.823.2525
Max Red/Blue, Washington Park Station

Take the last Red or Blue line to urban camp ("squat") underneath the stars. Get off at the Washington Park Max Station, trek up the hill and find the tree with the lowest limbs. Crawl into your sleeping bag and thank those stars you aren't staying at the Joyce Hotel. Though a phone number is listed above, you are squatting; therefore calling ahead is not advisable. (ML)

CHAPTER 5

FUN

Almost as important as finding a good hole-in-the-wall drinking establishment and a place with a bed to throw your bags, is how to enjoy Portland while you're here. This chapter outlines fun from one end of the spectrum to the other. You'll learn how to join a free pick-up sports league and where to go to borrow feminist literature. You'll skim over Skint's strip club recommendations for the financially challenged then read up on the shortcut to the horse track if you're arriving by foot. At the end of this section is a venue guide to use as a reference for finding the shows that are best suited for you. (ML)

fun

Recess Time Sports
Recesstimesports.com
Recess Time Sports is a website that organizes pick-up sports and leagues: namely bowling, kickball, dodge ball and ping pong. I wish I could be of more help here, but after Liz Lemon made a reference to ironic dodge ball leagues, any ambition I had to sign up for pick-up games to meet "weird" Portlanders went out the window. But maybe you're new to town and don't watch "30 Rock". Tell me how it goes. (ML)

DOWNTOWN

Fifth Avenue Cinema
5thavenuecinema.org
510 SW Hall St. 503.725.3551
$3 General Admission; $2 students and seniors; Free to PSU students.
Bus #1, 8, 12, 94, Max Yellow/Green, PSU Station
Fifth Avenue Cinema is one of the only university-run cinemas in the country, running camp, comedy and classics with unlimited popcorn on Fridays, Saturdays and Sundays. (ML)

Ground Kontrol
511 NW Couch St. 503.796.9364
Open daily 12pm-2:30am   After 5 pm, 21+
Max Yellow/Green, NW 6th and Davis Station
Ground Kontrol keeps Portland weird by following one simple rule: take something that everyone knows and loves (in this case, an arcade), and put a bar in it. Whether you play your best friend in "Street Fighter", or go after your old high score in "Pac-Man", a visit to this place is like reliving your childhood (except with a beer in hand instead of a slurpee). Most games cost only a quarter, so you can feel nostalgic about the price, too. On the first Wednesday and third Thursday of every month Ground Kontrol charges a five-dollar entry fee beginning at five o'clock. After the entry fee, all games are free until two in the morning. (IF)

Museum of Contemporary Craft

museumofcontemporarycraft.org

724 NW Davis St. 503.223.2654

Tues-Sat 11am-6pm

$3 Adults, $2 Students/Seniors

Free for children under 12 Free on First Thursdays

Bus #9, 17 Max Yellow/Green, NW Davis/Couch Station

Spending three dollars to stroll through craft collections may seem like the ideal way to pass an hour in downtown Portland, but be forewarned: this museum is only for the true craft enthusiast. Their exhibits are best suited for people with craft-extensive backgrounds—to common folk, the Museum of Contemporary Craft seems bland. (ML)

Portland Art Museum

1219 SW Park Ave. 503.226.2811

Mon - Closed. Tues-Wed 10am-5pm, Thurs-Fri 10am-5pm,

Sat 10am-5pm, Sun 12pm-5pm

$12 Adults; $9 College Students/Seniors, Free for children under 17

Bus #6, 38, 43, 45, Portland Streetcar

On the fourth Friday of every month from five to eight in the evening, the Portland Art Museum is free—and as such, very busy. If you're a student and plan on being in town a while, present a valid school ID and pay ten dollars for an Annual College Pass that gets you in free for the duration of the school year. (ML)

Rich's Cigar Shop

820 SW Alder St. 503.228.1700

Mon-Fri 8am-7pm, Sat 9am-6pm, Sun 10am-5pm   Ages 18+

Bus #20, Portland Streetcar, Max Red/Blue, Galleria Station

Because their tobacco and magazines are too expensive to purchase, Rich's Cigar Shop is best for browsing, reading and loitering—and apparently they've never kicked anyone out for doing so. They offer over 2,500 periodicals, so go ahead and read Polish Cuisine, Bat Fancy, or Delusional Bride cover to cover (or until the rain stops and you can go back outside). (ML)

art galleries | pearl district

After Ground Kontrol has eaten all your quarters, and you're searching for something to do, become acquainted with Portland's contemporary art scene. Galleries are a largely untapped resource of free culture in the downtown area. Skint recommends a visit to the following galleries.

GALLERIES

1
Butters Gallery
520 NW Davis St.

2
Froelick Gallery
714 NW Davis St.

3
Augen Gallerys Inc
716 NW Davis St.

4
Museum of
   Contemporary Craft
724 NW Davis St.

5
Charles A. Hartman
   Fine Art
134 NW 8th Ave.

6
Gallery 903
903 NW Davis St.

7
Blue Sky
122 NW 8th Ave.

8
Several galleries
   on one block
120 NW 9th Ave

9
Breeze Block Gallery
323 NW 6th Ave.

10
Low Brow Lounge
1036 NW Hoyt St.

NORTHWEST

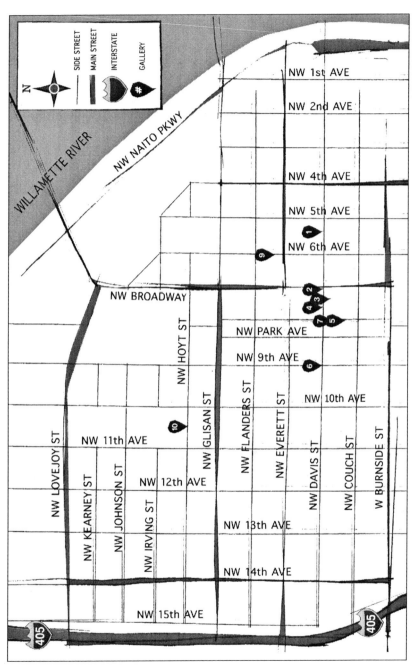

fun

The Bluffs
2206 N Skidmore St.
(Dead end of N Skidmore Terrace)
Max Yellow, North Prescott Station

A nightly migration occurs from the inner east neighborhoods to "the bluffs," a once top-secret spot now beloved by the young and rowdy. Folks bike and walk west on Skidmore Street until they hit its steep dead end. It feels like you're in someone's back yard, and you are—but it's also a legit city park: Mocks Crest Property. As the sun sets over the West Hills you have a truly romantic view of the city, the Willamette River and the Union Pacific train yard below. (MB)

Interstate Lanes
6049 N. Interstate Ave. 503.285.9881
Mon-Fri 10am-10pm, Sat-Sun 10am-12pm
Max Yellow, North Rosa Parks Station

When the urge strikes to knock things over with balls, visit Interstate Lanes, the semi-old-school, slightly tawdry neighborhood bowling alley, aplenty with neon, ugly murals, fried food and domestic beer out of plastic cups. It's a few bucks to wear the scuzzy shoes that so many have donned before, and the price per game varies by age, day, time, and league membership status. The thrifty bowler will head out for dollar games, available Sunday mornings from 10am-1pm and Tuesdays 10am-3pm. Avoid weekend nights unless you want to "rock and bowl" with pre-teens. (MB)

Kelley Point Park
N Marine Dr. & N Lombard St.
Open daily 6am-9pm
Bus #16

Originally intended to be a city by Hall Jackson Kelley, Kelley Point was acquired from the Port of Portland in 1984. Kelley Point is a quiet park with a beach bounded by the Columbia

Portland Meadows
crown prince...

Of all my favorite short people, Joe Crispin stands tall. Crispin, arguably Portland Meadows' winningest jockey, is something of a double-edged sword. Placing money on him is the surest bet, if there ever was one, but also one that yields the least return. He's such a successful jockey, it's foolish to bet against him. And many don't. This in turn gives him the best odds and the least payout when he wins the race. Best to use his odds in a Trifecta bet, where you can pair him with riskier odds and a bigger jackpot. Either way, I'm naming my first born son after him. (ML)

and Willamette River and the Columbia Slough. In summer, boysenberries are in abundance, novel for making some very local—yet unpalatable—wine. Also fun: going for a dip in the river, though upon reflection this might not be the best idea. (ML)

Portland Meadows

1001 N Schmeer Rd. 503.285.9144
Max Yellow, Vanport Station

Gambling is a serious problem but it's also a fucking blast—specifically when you're betting on ponies. From October through April at Portland Meadows, I set my animal activist-induced vegetarianism aside and scream at horses like they slapped my mother. The quickest and most unreliable way to win back the money you spent at the bar last night is to take the Max Yellow Line to the Vanport Station. Get off the train and walk down underneath the tracks along North Victory Boulevard, taking a right at North Whitaker Road. Walk along here and you'll see Portland Meadows off to the left—surrounded by a very scalable fence (which will cut your walking time in half). If you're wearing your Sunday Best to the track and don't want to snag anything, continue along and take a left at North Schmeer Road (there are no fence obstacles this way). Upon entering Portland Meadows, head to

Fun

FUN

the Information Desk and purchase a program. A few dollars will buy you all the information on horses, jockeys and races you need to know to make those safe, sound bets. (ML)

Widmer Brewery Tour

widmer.com

929 N Russell St. 503.281.2437

Fri 3pm, Sat 11am, 12:30pm   All ages, reservations necessary
          Bus #35, 85, Max Yellow, Albina/Mississippi Station

Widmer provides a mildy buzzed (free samples), informative tour of beer production, if you ignore that one asshole of the tour who thinks he invented the I-Love-Beer joke—the one that makes the old men dressed for urban hiking laugh. Each hour-long tour time boasts a different advantage. The Friday evening slot may be without the lame jokester still drunk from the night before, but during the Saturday tour, you'll be able to hear the tour guide, since the machines will be down. It's a crapshoot with a free (empty) Widmer pint at the end. (ML)

NORTHEAST

Bitch Lending Library

bitchmagazine.org/library

4930 NE 29th Ave.

Tues and Thurs 5pm-8pm
          Bus #72

Perusing books on sexuality and erotica is never as guilt-free as it is during the six-hour-a-week window that the Bitch Lending Library is open. Their collection of books, zines, DVDs and magazines is formidable and their lending practices are simple: present state-issued identification and take home that copy of "Sexier Sex" for two weeks. If it's a Tuesday, grab a vegan sweet on your way out. (ML)

Joseph Wood Hill Park

NE Rocky Butte Rd.

Open daily 5am-12am
          Bus #24 with 1.5 miles walking

Joseph Wood Hill Park rests atop Rocky Butte, an extinct volcanic cinder cone, whose grand height affords an awe-inspiring 360-degree vista of Oregon and Washington. Getting there through public transit can be a challenge, so it's best to convince a friendly car-owner of its scenic charm. (ML)

Kennedy School

mcmenamins.com/kennedyschool
5736 NE 33rd Ave. 503.249.3983
Soaking pool open daily 10am-10pm
> Bus #72

The enterprising McMenamins brothers transformed the grounds of an early twentieth century elementary school into a site of debauchery—converting classrooms into hotel rooms and janitors closets into tiny, cleverly titled bars (such as the "Detention Room" and the "Honors Room"). The real draws here are the second-run movie theater with cheap admission and couch seating, in addition to an outdoor Turkish-style soaking pool that you can access one of two ways: pay a few bucks or prove you live in the neighborhood, in which case they'll let you in free. See what you can do. (MB)

Last Thursday on Alberta Street

NE 15th Alberta St. to 30th Alberta St.
Last Thurs of every month, March-October
> Bus #72

Every last Thursday Northeast Alberta becomes a cattle call for citizens doing their darndest to "Keep Portland Weird." Vendors peddling crappy art, kitschy shit, and mediocre food cart fare line these fifteen city blocks. The real appeal: after dark, the street becomes a hotbed for various exhibitionists who come to perform for the captive audience in the hundreds of people streaming down the street. Expect stilts, tall bike parades, guitar strumming, culturally appropriated drumming circles, fortunetellers, fire-eaters, free hugs, and self-conscious performance art. (MB)

First Thursday in the Pearl

Monthly

> Max Green/Yellow, Davis/Couch Station

Last Thursday is a response to First Thursday, a snootier version of an art walk, where the galleries in the Pearl debut new exhibits. Last Thursday is packed with suburbanites, weirdos and kitsch art—all with a flare for the bohemian. This Alberta Walk may seem more up your alley, but you will get way more drunk at First Thursday, where the wine and beer flows freely to celebrate artists and galleries who cannot begin to comprehend how highly you revere free alcohol. (ML)

Forest Park

NW 29th Ave. and NW Upshur to Newbury Rd.

Open daily 5am-10pm

> Bus not advisable

Providing the jagged Evergreen outline at the western end of Portland, Forest Park is the largest, most unimaginatively named natural urban area in the nation. The park has thirty miles of trails intended for use by hikers, horses and cyclists. The old growth park is home to over a hundred species of birds and over sixty mammals. Forest Park is completely contained within city limits, making it simple to experience both the wilderness and the city life in a single day. (ML)

Vaux's Swifts

1445 NW 26th Ave.

"Most Evenings" in September at dusk

> Bus #15, 77

In September, many thousands of birds, namely *chaetura vauxi* (Vaux's Swifts) make the out-sized chimney at Chapman School their home. In preparation for their winter trip to Venezuela, these creatures gorge on Portland's abundant insect population before returning at dusk in a great, chattering, fractal gyre only to vanish suddenly into the flue. It's quite the aerial spectacle—

Fun

a fact which hasn't been lost on Portland's particular breed of picnic parent. So be prepared to hear endless, pointless exhortations in the tiniest of voices to "look... look at the birds..." I mention the last detail as a service to our readers knowing the Skint stratum's proclivity for drunken debauchery. (JB)

SOUTHEAST

Burnside Skatepark
Under the Burnside Bridge at SE 2nd Ave
　　Bus #6, 12, 19, 20
The Portland skating community built the infamous Burnside skatepark in 1990 and it was only later sanctioned by the city. The skate park, which is public, free and has no pad requirements, is featured in "Tony Hawk's Pro Skater" video game. In order for this virtual skate park to be a more accurate representation, it would have to be much smaller, surrounded by homeless people, drug dealers and slags. Depending on the skater, the park may be a seedy underbelly or a raucous good time. (ML)

Mt Tabor Park
SE 60th Ave. and SE Salmon St.
Open daily 5am-12am
　　Bus #4, 15, 71
Mt Tabor Park, noteworthy for its location atop a volcanic cinder cone, provides some of the most arresting views of the city. The park is equally worth the visit day or night, when the lights of the city in the valley dazzle against the trees and mountains of the west side. (ML)

Wunderland/The Avalon
wunderlandgames.com
3451 SE Belmont St. 503.238.1617
Sun-Fri 12am-12pm, Sat 11am-12am　　　Cash only
　　Bus #15
Arcades don't get more classic than Wunderland, which comes

fun

complete with blinking lights and creepy clowns. Proudly billed as a "Portland tradition since 1936," this arcade is a trip through games of the past seventy years, with Skee ball alongside "Bunk Hunter II" and everything in between. Adult admission is $2.50 and each game is then two to three nickels per play, all with the chance to earn tickets to cash in for some kitschy shit. Keychains! The Avalon, the second-run theater next door, sells tickets from $2.50 to $3 and shows movies all day. (MB)

SOUTHWEST

Aerial Tram
3303 SW Bond Ave.
Mon-Fri 5:30am-9:30pm, Sat 9am-5pm, Sun 1pm-5pm
      Portland Streetcar
The aerial tram is the poor man's helicopter ride—that is, a helicopter ride that just goes back in forth in one straight line at 3300 feet in the air—and at a fraction of the price: four dollars. It doesn't get you anywhere convenient, unless you're at the waterfront and are utilizing your degree in medical coding and billing at Oregon Health & Science University. The aerial tram provides the cheapest, highest public transit option in Portland. (ML)

International Rose Test Garden
400 SW Kingston Ave.
Open daily 7:30am-9pm
      Bus #63, Max Red/Blue, Goose Hollow/SW Jefferson Station
After screwing up royally with your girlfriend, do not go by yourself to the International Rose Test Garden to pick a bouquet out of the five hundred and fifty varieties of roses. Doing so carries a hefty fine. Instead, bring her along for a quiet stroll through the garden's seven thousand rosebushes and admire the amazing vistas while you explain to her that you don't know who wrote her sister's name on your dick, took a picture of it, and sent it to her sister's phone—but you did try to rub it off as fast as you could while thinking of her. (ML, Casey Harris)

Oregon Zoo

oregonzoo.org
4001 SW Canyon Rd. 503.226.1561 ext. 0
Open daily, typically 10am-4pm
        Max Red/Blue, Washington Park Station
$10.50 Adults, $9 Seniors, $7.50 Children ages 3-11
On the second Tuesday of every month, you can see lions, tigers and bears at the Oregon Zoo at discounted tickets only four dollars a pop. On any other day, you can save a dollar-fifty off the standard ticket price if you present your Trimet ticket. (ML)

Zoobomb

zoobomb.net
Corner of SW 13th and Burnside
Sun-8:30pm
        Bus #20
One does not have to be a zoobomber to participate in this iconic Portland bicycle event. For eight years, people of every ilk gathered at the corner of SW 13th and Burnside at 8:30 pm every Sunday, in order to jump on the Max to the Zoo and ride a mini bike down one of the steep hills surrounding the Oregon Zoo Max Station in Washington Park. A distinctive aroma, overt sexuality, and sophomoric rebellion are not required here; one should, however, expect Che references, ribaldry, and a certain amount of funk on the ride up. (JB)

strip clubs

There are more strip clubs in Portland per capita than in any other city in the U.S. This may be related to our location just five miles South of Washington, a state opposed to the display of the unclad vagina. This dearth of strip clubs is definitely facilitated by the 1987 ruling of *Henry v. the Oregon Constitution*, which protects full nudity and lap dances as expressions of free speech. The supreme court decision reflects Oregon's status as a refuge for grown-ups who can make up their own minds about the "vulgarity" of the human form, unlike a certain commonwealth to the North. So hit the club and enjoy these rights in Oregon. First the facts and rules: strippers are not paid wages. In fact, they pay to dance. So tip, fucker. When at the rack (the seats nearest the stage) don't eat—it's rude—and tip every song—it's ruled. Memorize the three "L's." First, these women are ladies. They are mothers and daughters, not weird objects for you to touch, proposition, or creep out. Second, they are laborers—this is their job, frequently 40 hours a week. You are in their place of employment—respect that. Third, love. No, they don't love you, they're working. Remember that someone who is "out of line" at a strip club universally translates as "piece of shit," so err on the side of caution and class and have a good time.

Furthermore, when interested in a lap dance, find the lady offstage and ask her for a "private dance," which usually costs twenty dollars. After she leads you into the back room, your dancer will inform you of her rules. Some performers are comfortable with light touching, but frequently, dancers will not even touch you. This is normal. You have not been ripped off. This is a lap dance in a progressive city full of working professionals, so keep your hat on, Jed. (JB)

Acropolis Steakhouse

8325 SE McLoughlin Blvd. 503.231.9611

Mon-Sat 7am-2:30pm, Sun 11am-2:30am

Bus #31, 32, 33

A piece of gossip: when Marilyn Manson is in town, he goes to this strip club-cum-steakhouse in deep Southeast, thus illustrating a Portland land maxim: the outskirts have the best deals. "The Acrop" (as it's called by the townies), boasts five-dollar pitchers, fifty-one beers on tap and a five-dollar steak breakfast. The club has three stages, no cover before four-thirty in the evening, and some of the friendliest staff in town (for the money). Go for brunch, otherwise you'll end up paying the cover, having three too many, missing the bus, and blowing what's left of your cash on a cab back to civilization. (JB)

Mary's Club

129 SW Broadway 503.227.3023

Mon-Sat 11am-2:30am, Sun 11:30am-2:30am

Bus #1, 12, 19, 20, 54, 56

Max Yellow/Green, SW 6th and Pine or SW 5th and Oak Station

As the oldest topless club in Portland, Mary's has achieved a certain singularity of purpose. The place is a loud, dark, narrow corridor with rows of seats facing a single stage on which women dance and you pay up. To ensure this, Mary's employs time-tested methods: Friday and Saturday there's a two dollar cover, a one drink minimum, and strippers ask for the money to play songs on the jukebox during their own dances. It's popular when you find yourself downtown, chaperoning first timers, or when you're in need of Mexican food: the adjoining restaurant (shared bathrooms) is quite good. (JB)

Sassy's

927 SE Morrison St. 503.231.1606

Open daily 11am-2am

Bus #15, 70

You can go to the Holocene, if only to see the hipsters (who are your friends) between stalwart bands in a five-plus-dollar beer environment, or you can go next door to Sassy's. When

strip clubs

strip clubs

I envision strip clubs—like when I'm dreaming—this one always pops into my head. Sassy's is the quintessential strip club. There's no cover, cheap Olympia tall boys, food that's palatable, three stages, and an outdoor smoking patio, as well as the most beautiful dancers in P-town. (JB)

Silverado

318 SW 3rd Ave. 503.224.4493
Open daily 9am-2:30am
        Bus #15, 51

In a city so rife with undressing mothers and daughters, there are surprisingly few clubs offering work for the fathers and sons of stripper families, making this gay (owned and supported) strip club in the heart of downtown all the more vital, relevant and essential. There's dancing about six nights a week (call ahead to check), strong drinks, cheap food, and free condoms. It gets a bit raunchy in the evenings, reflecting its twofold role as a club both gay and strip. (JB)

venues

Portland plays host to a number of shows at a menagerie of different venues on any given night. The following reviews of Rose City venues provide some insight into what to expect from that show you saw on a flier, in the Willamette Week, or heard about on the bus. Is the show at one of those big venues that require you to do some pre-show drinking because they exclusively serve pricey cocktails in plastic cups? Or is at a small, intimate affair at a bar that only hosts bluegrass? Knowing what to expect from the venue will help you come in under budget at the end of the night. (ML)

Aladdin Theater
aladdin-theater.com
3017 SE Milwaukee Ave. 503.234.9694   Some shows all ages, 21+
          Bus #9, 19, 66, 17, 70
The Aladdin Theater is a mid-sized, seated venue with expensive tickets. Stay in for two nights in order to save up enough money to watch your favorite band from the '90s play here. (ML)

Ash Street Saloon
ashstreetsaloon.com
225 SW Ash St. 503.226.0430   Shows 21+
          Bus #12, 19, 20
The stage is too high, the room is too big, and the drinks are too pricey. But they'll probably let your band play here—meaning they regularly host mediocre local bands. The bar next door, Captain Ankeny's Well, is also pricey but they offer cheap slices of pizza. (ML)

Backspace Cafe
backspace.biz
115 NW 5th Ave.   All Ages
          Max Yellow/Green, NW Davis/Couch Station
Coffee shop by day, venue by night, Backspace usually showcases rock bands and hosts a small and average-priced selection of beers. Best to

venues

enjoy the Scooter McQuade's (page 22) happy hour up the street before returning to the show. (ML)

Branx

myspace.com/branxpdx
320 SE 2nd Ave.
Bus #6, 15

Branx is the dirty little secret in Rotture's basement. You'll find bumping glitchy beats and fabulous dancers—I saw a huge, bearded dude dropping it, in matching corset and thong. This is an ideal place to get sweaty, although you might not be able to afford replenishing fluids because the cocktails are so expensive. It's bathroom sink or bust. (IF)

Crystal Ballroom

mcmenamins.com/425-crystal-ballroom-home
1332 W Burnside St. 503.225.0047   Shows all ages and 21+
Bus #20

At the Crystal Ballroom the little kids are separated from the adults by a blockade to accommodate all age shows. On the adult side of the fence you can purchase expensive drinks, but on both sides you can bounce on the rubber floor that gives. (ML)

Dante's

danteslive.com
350 W Burnside St. 503.226.6630   Shows 21+
Bus #9, 12, 19, 22, 17, 54, 56 Max Yellow/
Green, NW Davis/Couch Station

Dante's is a medium-sized venue, meaning the stage is going to be just a little too high, the beers are going to be just a little too expensive, but you'll get to watch a band that you're not already friends with. (ML)

Doug Fir Lounge

dougfirlounge.com
830 E Burnside St. 503.231.WOOD   Shows 21+
Bus #12, 19, 20

The Doug Fir is the antithesis of a dive bar. Wait in long lines for bottles of Miller High Life in the cleanest environment you've

ever blacked out in. Do NOT throw glassware at the Doug Fir.
On a related note, Bob Log III: please stop playing here. (ML)

Dunes

myspace.com/dunesportland

1909 NE Martin Luther King Jr. Blvd. 503.493.8637   Shows 21+
        Bus #4, 6, 9, 44

Dunes is a hard-to-find hole-in-the-wall presenting off-the-wall
shows—and expensive drinks—so arrive drunk. Or, just hit up
Billy Ray's between sets. (ML)

East End

eastendpdx.com

203 SE Grand Ave. 503.232.0056   Shows 21+
        Bus #6

The East End regularly hosts good shows with solid local bands
and more national acts. However, the beer is expensive and the
line you'll bump into in the bathroom might not be able to counter this. (ML)

The Goodfoot

thegoodfoot.com

2845 SE Stark St. 503.239.9292   Shows 21+
        Bus #15

The Goodfoot hosts a lot of shows throughout the week, so
show up, stink like Nag Champa and let your hair down while
you dance fluidly with no regard to rhythm. (ML)

Hawthorne Theatre

hawthornetheatre.com

1507 SE 39th Ave.   Shows all ages and 21+
        Bus #14, 66, 75

The Hawthorne Theatre is a venue with big names that isn't
worth the big hassle. There's no re-entry into the place, and
the bathroom has only one stall. Kids in the front; adults in the
back. Best bet is to stay outside, be over twenty-two, smoke ciga-
rettes and pretend to be on your way to Fred Meyer while scam-
ming a listen. (ML)

venues

venues

Holocene
holocene.org
1001 SE Morrison St. 503.239.7639   Shows 21+
Bus #15, 70.
You go to the Holocene to be seen, not to see the band. (ML)

Hungry Tiger Too
myspace.com/hungrytigertoo
207 SE 12th Ave. 503.238.4321   Shows 21+
        Bus #12, 19, 20, 70
The louder-than-shit shows at Hungry Tiger Too always seem like an obstacle to those who equate the bar with cheap vegan corn dogs. Cheap vegan fare aside, typically this place showcases talented local bands. Block the Facebook and swear off texting before consuming the All-Day-Sipper to avoid any apologies you might need to make the next morning for your behavior the night before. (ML)

The Knife Shop
kellysolympian.com
426 SW Washington St. 503.228.3669
Shows 21+
        Bus #4, 15, 31, 32, 33, 51
        Max Yellow/Green, Pioneer
Square Station
The Knife Shop consistently offers mediocre shows and an unfriendly staff. (ML)

Mississippi Studios
mississippistudios.com
3939 N Mississippi Ave. 503.288.3895
Shows 21+
        Bus #4
Mississippi Studios, benefiting from a recent renovation, has been praised for being one of the most intimate venues in Portland, with an

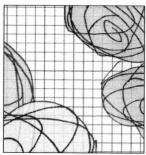

LOUD
bands in
living rooms...

The best resource for finding a show outside of the bar realm is **pc-pdx.com**. Go to page 90 for more details.

excellent sound system and skillful sound technicians. If a band you like is playing there, which is rare for me—go. (ML)

Mudai Lounge

twitter.com/mudailounge
801 NE Broadway St. 503.287.5433   Shows 21+
      Bus #9, 77

As Chinese restaurants in Portland have welcomed karaoke into their hearts, so too have Ethiopian restaurants welcomed rock 'n' roll. Mudai Lounge is a prime example of this: an attentive staff serves up a limited bar in a simple, yet charming atmosphere. (ML)

Plan B

dbmonkey.com/planb
1305 SE 8th Ave.   Shows 21+
      Bus #10, 14

Plan B is where the kids from Burnside Skatepark go for a change of scenery. (MB)

Roseland Theater

roselandpdx.com
8 NW 6th Ave. 503.224.2038   Some shows 21+
      Bus #1, 4, 8, 9, 12, 17, 19, 20, 54
      Max Yellow/Green, Couch/Davis Station

There's a distinctive entry process at the Roseland Theater: first, get molested by the security guards and wait in line to pass through unnecessary metal detectors; then, buy a round of over-priced drinks; finally, spend the whole time moping because your favorite band (who hasn't been in town for two years) decided to play one of Portland's worst venues, rather than the similarly-depressing and barely-superior Cyrstal Ballroom. Since the live music experience sucks, enjoy watching the bouncers beat up on pot-smokers. (IF)

venues

venues

Rotture

rotture.com

315 SE 3rd Ave.

Bus #6

Rotture is located in the industrial area of Portland that reminds you of the desolate areas of your native city—the one you left in order to move here. The drinks are expensive, but, shit, I saw Thee Oh Sees play on the second-story smoking patio—and I didn't die,—so I'm going back. (ML)

Saratoga

6910 N Interstate Ave. 503.719.5924

Max Yellow, North Rosa Parks Station

Indicative of the young crowd moving into North Portland, Saratoga—the newest neighborhood flip—serves the tastes of their clientele well. Vintage neon beer signs line the flat black walls that offer pinball and the menu features a portabella mushroom sandwich. They have a stage that is well-suited for bands, but this place lacks proper sound proofing in a residential area, which hampers late night shows. (ML)

Slabtown

slabtownbar.net

1033 NW 16th Ave. 503.223.0099

Bus #77, Portland Streetcar

In the 1850s the Northwest side of town was called "Slabtown," so dubbed because "if you went there, you'd end up on a slab." Things are a bit tamer now under the Fremont bridge, but it still has a rebellious appeal that gives this bar its M.O. This place was once the known hangout of self-aggrandizing local band the Dandy Warhols and their posse, and now its new owners are bringing in a fledgling generation of wannabe rock 'n roll ers with shows, DJs and a dank dive atmosphere. With over a dozen pinball machines, a greasy menu and a loaded jukebox, Slabtown will keep you feeling that the world's still dangerous and that rock still kills. (MB)

Someday Lounge

somedaylounge.com

125 NW 5th Ave. 503.248.1030   Shows 21+

    Bus #4, 8, 9, 16, 33, 35, 44

    Max Yellow/Green, Davis/Couch Station

Someday Lounge is overly hipster swank, though the sound system bumps and the Old German is cheap. Funk nights are what the place was made for; check out the Dookie nights (funk jam sessions). (IF)

venues

CHAPTER 6

EAT

Skint scoured to find the diners, bars and food carts with the most menu items under six dollars, paying special attention to breakfast. More than a couple establishments around town offer the popular eggs, hash browns and toast special at a reasonable price. The Cheerful Tortoise and Cheerful Bullpen do indeed have the best deal in town at under two dollars. The other diners and bars work their way up in price from there, capping off at the aforementioned six dollars. (ML)

BREAKFAST

eat

Cheerful Tortoise
1939 SW 6th Ave. 503.224.3377
Mon-Fri 7am-2am, Sat-Sun 9am-2pm   21+ only
    Bus #1, 8, 9, 12, 17, 19, 35, 36, 43, 44, 94
    Max Green/Yellow, PSU Station

Cheerful Bullpen
1730 SW Taylor St. 503.222.3063
Mon-Fri 11am-2am, Sat-Sun 9am-2am   21+ only
    Bus #15, 18, 51, 63 Max Red/Blue, Kings Hill Station
So what if you don't like watching college sports on 612 televisions? So what if you can't stand Muzak? So what if you like windows? Both the Cheerful Tortoise and its sister dive—the Cheerful Bullpen—offer two eggs, toast and hash browns for a dollar-ninety-nine all day, everyday. It's not listed on the menu, but they have it: just ask. (ML)

Corner Spot Tavern
6008 N Greeley Ave. 503.285.1035
Mon-Sat 11am-Late
    Bus #35
The Corner Spot Tavern is desolate to those under forty years old, and home to those over fifty years old. But even desolation is tolerable when coupled with a breakfast featuring eggs, toast and hash browns for only two and a half dollars. It's not listed on the menu, but if you ask for it specifically, the bartender will make it for you. (ML)

John's Cafe
301 NW Broadway St. 503.227.4611
Open Mon-Fri 7am-3pm   Cash only
    Bus #19
The simple menu reflects the simple food and the coffee is merely palatable, but you don't go to John's for any certain menu item. You go to get full for cheap. You go to hear the stories the owners tell about how the intersection of Broadway

eat

and Everett has changed over the past twenty years. You go to avoid the typical Portland breakfast eaters who expect their orange juice fresh-squeezed and their bacon to be from Carlton Farms. The experience is plenty worth the three dollars and change you're going to spend on breakfast. (ML)

Kelly's Olympian
426 SW Washington St. 503.228.3669
Open daily 10am-2:30am   21+ only
    Bus #4, 15, 31, 32, 33, 51
    Max Green/Yellow, Pioneer Square Station
Kelly's Olympian serves four-dollar breakfast (eggs, hash browns and toast) all day and night—and is even cheaper after midnight, if suffering from insomnia, jet lag or drunken cravings. (ML)

Leo's Nonsmoking Coffee Shop
837 SE 11th Ave. 503.228.1866
Mon-Fri 7am-3pm   Cash only
    Max Red/Blue, Central Library Station
Put your love of diner kitsch to the test at Leo's Nonsmoking Coffee Shop, where you'll encounter Portland's most charming restaurant owner. He's the only waiter in the joint, yet he's still got time to amass a two foot stack of newspaper at your table, and then apologize profusely after you ask for ketchup. The place looks amazing (pearly white counters with blue accents), and the food is decent. It's a dining experience set in a backdrop to a David Lynch film. (IF)

Marathon Taverna
1735 W Burnside St. 503.224.1341
Open daily 7am-2am
    Bus #20
Visit for the two-dollar breakfast (eggs, bacon and toast available until two in the afternoon) and stay for the opportunity to "Kill the Keg"—pints of Busch are only a dollar until the keg is gone. The Marathon Taverna is yet another bar on Burnside with fake wood walls and blue-collar regulars, but, this one—channels its inner hardware store—with free popcorn. (ML)

eat

Tabor Hill Café
3766 SE Hawthorne Blvd. 503.230.1231
Open daily 8am–9pm
　　Bus #14

Tabor Hill Café is the best place in Southeast to read the paper. Here you'll find standard diner chum: pleasant in that quaint, family-run business kind of way. The café is easily the calmest place to get weekend breakfast around Hawthorne. I don't know what they do to the orange juice to make it so frothy, but try not to think too much about it. To stay on the cheap side, avoid the lunch and dinner menus and stick to the breakfast fare served all day. (IF)

Tom's Restaurant
3871 SE Division St. 503.233.3739
Open daily 9am-9:30pm
　　Bus #4, 75

While it may not offer the cheapest breakfast special around, Tom's does have a few things going for it. In a largely yuppified swath of Portland, Tom's is a throwback to a more frugal-minded time. The eggs, bacon, French toast, and an orange slice is a solid deal. Throw in Tom's early morning hours—the Lounge opens at seven in the morning for the old-man-graveyard-hours crowd (who might otherwise suffer their morning booze alone if not for this bastion of the drinking class)—and you've got a stellar little diner with consistently mediocre service. (CR)

DOWNTOWN

Alexandrya
420 SW College St. 503.222.3922
Mon-Fri 11am-7pm
　　Bus #1, 8, 12, 17, 44, 94
　　Max Yellow/Green Line, PSU Station

Alexandrya is an unassuming restaurant tucked into Portland State's campus. Two brothers spend eight hours a day serving up Lebanese fare at ridiculously fair prices. (ML)

eat

Bombay Chaat House

804 SW 12th Ave. 503.380.3087

Mon-Sat 10am-7pm.   Cash only

Bus #15, 51, Max Red/Blue, Central Library Station,

Portland Streetcar

It's as though the numerous Indian food carts in town see only other Indian food carts as their sole competition. Thus, each cart has driven down market prices, landing steadily at the six-dollar lunch special. Since the playing field has been leveled, make taste your deciding factor and choose Bombay Chaat House. Their mutter paneer knows no rival and they always throw in free Chai. (ML, JB)

Hope's Deli

120 SW Jefferson St. 503.224.4247

Mon-Fri 6am-4:30pm

Bus #38, 45, 55, 92, 96

Bleak walls and fluorescent lighting welcome you into one of the cheapest eateries in downtown Portland. Hope's Deli offers a menu that any frugal asshole can get excited over: burgers, bento and breakfast (if you arrive before ten-thirty in the morning), and not one item is over six dollars. Jack of all trades, Ace of none? No worries, they sell Tums at the end of the counter. (ML)

Jefferson's Pizza Restaurant

1221 SW Jefferson St. 503.241.2431

Open daily 11:10am-4:45am

Bus #6

Cheap slices and pies at odd prices ($6.66, $7.77 $8.88 and so on) are available from this little restaurant tucked into a crevice on SW Jefferson Street. Jefferson's Pizza is open until early in the morning—quarter to five, to be exact—so stumble in after the bars close to purchase a cheap snack you won't remember eating with money you won't notice is missing. (ML)

eat

Sisters of the Road Cafe
133 NW 6th Ave. 503.222.5694
Mon-Fri 10am-2pm
> Max Yellow/Green, NW 6th and Davis Station
> Bus #4, 8, 9, 12, 17, 20, 33, 35

By eating at this place for the first time, you're essentially cashing in the last Portland "chip" you have. Maybe you're a transient looking to get out of Portland pretty soon, or maybe you're leaving rehab and starting the hard road to recovery. The first meal (five dollars or less) is free when you sign up for a time-slot (which you're able to do as early as nine in the morning), but after that, you have to start paying in cash, EBT, or labor; it's pretty much one of the last "free rides" you can get in a city full of them. That said, five bucks is enough for two people, and is made with the healthiest, most organic ingredient of them all: love. (JB)

NORTH

East Side Delicatessen
4823 N Lombard Ave. 503.247.3354
Open daily 11am-10pm
> Bus #4, 17, 44, 75

See page 74 for summary.

King Burrito
2924 N Lombard St. 503.283.9757
Open daily 10am-11pm
> Bus #35, 75

This North Portland institution serves the best breakfast burrito in town, but you should eat it without getting too fancy. This is because King Burrito is not a "Mexican food" place where people swear by the pork like Porque No?, it's a Mexican "food place" which is packed after Mass, serves menudo on weekends, and caters to a community whose preferred foods include indelicately seasoned lengua, tripa and sesos served floating in grease. Locals swear by the "King Burrito," an option only for old hands well versed in emergency bowel evacuation procedure. (JB)

eat

Santa Cruz
8630 N Lombard St. 503.285.8222
Open daily 9am-9pm
> Bus #4

This taquería hidden inside a tienda hidden in St. Johns has remained obscured for too long. Upon arrival walk straight through the grocery store in to the back, where stark, white walls and high ceilings house taquería Santa Cruz, where the flavors are rich and the guacamole is free. (ML)

NORTHEAST

The Black Cat Cafe
1203 NE Alberta St. 503.287.5908
Mon-Fri 6am-8pm, Sat-Sun 7am-8pm
> Bus #72

Toward the back of every edition of the city's weekly rag The Portland Mercury, you'll find an ad for the Black Cat promising a free bagel with any coffee purchase. Redeem this at what is one of the most laid-back and least pretentious cafes in town, despite their enormous selection of fair-trade, organic coffee. Chalk it up to the near permanent population of crusty street kids and their dogs who have taken up residence on the front sidewalk. Get cheap beer (on tap or to go), and 10 minutes of computer use costs a quarter. (MB)

Black Sheep Bakery
523 NE 19th Ave. 503.517.5762
Mon-Fri 7am-4pm, Sat 9am-2pm
> Bus #12, 19, 20

The Black Sheep Bakery—with one location tucked into Sandy Blvd., like a piece of bacon into a hamburger—is a pleasant and super vegan-friendly café. I recommend you build your own sandwich and get a side of gravy,—which is more like a soup, but a totally better vegan gravy than most. The hummus, pickles, and homemade, organic items seal the deal. (JB)

eat

La Sirenita

2817 NE Alberta St. 503.335.8283

Open daily 10am-10pm

   Bus #72

For Mexican food on Northeast Alberta Street, head to La Sirenita, where they don't put peas and carrots in their rice (like Don Poncho down the street) and they aren't too expensive (like La Bonita's next door). (ML)

Panera Cares Café

4121 NE Halsey St. 503.287.5900

   Bus # 12, 66, 75, 77

   Max Red/Blue/Green, Hollywood Max Station

Panera Cares Café is the pay-what-you-can version of the artisan sandwich chain, Panera's. There is a suggested donation in lieu of a price for the meal, so you pay what you can (want) to get the soup or sandwich you need (want). Panera's is operating under a new business model that plays on liberal guilt to keep the boat afloat; the theory is: if others pay more, you can pay less. Do what your hunger pangs tell you is just. (ML)

NORTHWEST

Eat Pizza!

Corner of W Burnside and 20th Pl. 503.243.3663

Open daily 10am-12am

   Bus #20

Skip the sandwiches. Skip the salads. Skip the appetizers and desserts. Instead, get the everyday option of the mini-ten-inch-plate-size-six-dollar pizza version of any specialty pizza on their menu—or make your own pie with unlimited toppings for the same six dollars. Chow down in their sliver of a restaurant then head up a few blocks to the Goodwill to bulk up your VHS collection. (ML)

eat

SOUTHEAST

An Xuyen Bakery

5345 SE Foster Rd. 503.788.0866

Tues-Sat 7am-6pm, Sun 7am-3pm

Bus #9, 14, 71

An Xuyen Bakery has the best pastries and sandwiches in the Foster/Powell neighborhood. Not sure how they keep their prices so low, but I'll ask after I finish stuffing my fat face with orgasmically sweet cakes and cookies. Less than three dollars for a good sandwich on fresh bread—so hey, Fatty, get two: no one's watching. (IF)

Black Sheep Bakery

833 SE Main St. 503.473.8534

Mon-Fri 7am-4pm, Sat 9am-2pm

Bus #10, 14

See page 72 for summary.

East Side Delicatessen

4626 SE Hawthorne Blvd. 503.236.7313

Open daily 11am-11pm

Bus #14

On one particular corner in Southeast, you'll find the Holy Trinity of everything it is to be a Portlander. On this divine corner on Hawthorne, you can find booze (Hawthorne Liquor Store), music (Exiled Records), and filling, inexpensive food in the form of fat fucking sandwiches at the East Side Delicatessen. The deli is fabulous for meat eaters, and kind to vegetarians (I hope you like imitation meat). (ML)

Food Not Bombs

Locations vary; email pdxfnb@lists.riseup.net
or foodnotbombs.net/oregon.html for details

Be forewarned that the intentionally badly dressed hipsters who attend Portland area Food Not Bombs Dinners for the experience and thrift outnumber any actual homeless/needy people in attendance. Nonetheless, you can eat here free every day of the week at five-thirty in the evening. While there, you will undoubtedly meet many people who will invite you to other hip events, like quirky movie nights or midnight bike rides. (MB)

eat

Good Neighbor
4107 SE 82nd Ave. 503.771.5171
Open daily 7am-9pm
    Bus #10, 14, 72
There's nowhere else in town to find more authentic Eastern European meats and cheeses as those you'll find at the small Russian deli, Good Neighbor, nestled in the never-ending strip-mall that is 82nd Avenue. You'll have to work hard, however, to get your hands on their meats—unless you speak Russian, expect communication problems with the store clerks. Perfect your pronunciation of Russian numbers and point clearly at the display case for the best results. (IF)

Pizza Ultimania
3508 SE 52nd Ave. 503.774.9929
Mon-Thurs 11am-10 pm, Fri-Sat 11am-11pm, Sun 11am-9pm
    Bus # 9, 14, 71
On desperate nights, find the warm fluorescent glow of Pizza Ultimania, Southeast's shining beacon of cheap, no-nonsense nourishment. Don't order off the menu: just hit up the takeout deals. Sure, the name might sound like it's the last pizza you'll ever eat—and sometimes, it tastes that way—but for the price, they can't be beat. (IF)

The Red & Black Café
400 SE 12th Ave. 503.231.3899
Open daily 9am–11pm   Cash only
    Bus #70
Whether you deem it a meeting place for the politically marginalized (read: anarchist) or, simply, a pool of pretentiousness, the Red and Black Café's long, cheap vegan menu leaves little to protest. (ML)

eat

Sivalai Thai Restaurant

4806 SE Stark St. 503.230.2875

Open daily 11am-10pm, lunch specials weekdays until 3pm

Bus #15

Sivalai Thai Restaurant is notorious for its crazy owner: he greets customers with a high-pitched welcome, and does dance moves as he takes your order. I suspect he keeps the entire cocaine trade afloat in Portland. As for the food: the menu prices may seem steep, but the free appetizer veggie rolls, Thai iced tea or coffee, and sticky rice with mango make for an affordable feast. It's best to split main courses among friends. (IF)

St. Francis Soup Kitchen

1131 SE Oak St. 503.232.5880

Meals served Mon-Fri 5:30pm, Sun 3:30pm

Bus # 70

Beggars can't be choosers, but you could do worse than a meal at St. Francis Soup Kitchen. Enjoy a hot, free serving of starches and grains with down-and-outers, served with a side order of what organizers promise with every meal: "dignity and peace." (MB)

Super Torta

5640 SE Woodstock Blvd. 503.788.3650

Open daily 9:30am-9:30pm

Bus #19, 71

I know you prefer to get your Mexican fix from food carts, but while you were waiting in line in the cold and rain for an over-priced burrito, I was sitting comfortably inside the colorful, kitsch-covered walls of Super Torta. Food served on red plastic cafeteria trays, horchata and jamaica bubbling in the drink machines: this is the authentic Mexican-American dining experience. (IF)

Wong's King

8733 SE Division St. 503.788.883

Mon-Fri 10am-11pm, Sat-Sun 9:30am-11pm

Bus #4

Arguably the best Chinese food in Portland, Wong's King boasts a mighty dim sum service. Waiters push steaming-hot buns and dumplings to your table on large carts and stack the plates ceremoniously on your lazy susan. Make it for the daily dim sum lunch, but avoid the dinner hours—the food is still delicious but the prices are hard to swallow. (IF)

Zach's Shack

4611 SE Hawthorne Blvd. 503.233.4616

Open daily 11am-3am

Bus #4, 14

When meandering down Hawthorne at midnight with your now empty Brass Monkey Slurpee, stumble into Zach's Shack for a hot dog. They have messy, inventive toppings (cole slaw, cheese, bacon) and they're open late. Or head in earlier to watch the game while filling your gut with creative American fare. (ML, IF)

CHAPTER 7

SPEND

Shopping for material possessions is the quickest way to blow through your money and weigh down your suitcase, but sometimes clothes get lost, shoes wear out and toothpaste doesn't pay for itself. If you must spend money, it's probably going to be on clothes, music, and books. For clothing, no boutiques are recommended here: only the cream-of-the-crop thrift shops that are not picked-over and are reasonable in price. We know that records are heavy in the bag, but necessary to life; therefore, Skint has listed here almost every vinyl store in Portland (expensive shops included), so you can be privy to their selection before heading out. And, finally, we've provided a list of independent bookstores with an alternative slant or those worth browsing in Portland: from the enormous Powell's, to the densely packed Cameron's. (ML)

SHOPS

spend

Bearly Worn Resale Store

4926 SE Division St. 503.252.0063

Wed-Sun 11am-6pm ($5 Store)

Fri-Sat 11am-6pm ($1 Warehouse)

> Bus #4, 14

Pop into the Bearly Worn Resale Store to peruse the barely-picked-over used items. Like Goodwill, the store sells second-hand hip sweaters, ugly sweaters, and hip, ugly sweaters— and not just sweaters: faded black v-neck three-quarter length sleeve shirts, dark blue denim Wranglers, as well as shoes from American Eagle that could pass for retro, in addition to a thousand other items. Unlike Goodwill, they have a five-dollar store (the hours listed for Wednesday through Sunday) and a special one-dollar warehouse (the Friday/Saturday hours above) where everything costs a fiver or a single, respectively. (ML)

The Bins

1740 SE Ochoco St., Milwaukie 503.230.2076

Mon-Sat 8am-8pm, Sun 9am-7pm

> Bus #35

This is used-goods shopping at its most chaotic, unhygienic, and cutthroat—yet unbeatably, unbelievably, cheap. "The Bins" contains the leftovers of what regional Goodwill stores weren't able to sell. In other words, it's a warehouse jam-packed with bins of crazy unorganized shit that's often broken or soiled. Plus, bargain-mongers are on the prowl, ready to pounce on a desirable item at any cost. Come prepared for this, and with plenty of time, and you may walk away with some serious treasure—yours for a dollar-fifty-nine a pound. (MB)

Black Rose Collective Bookstore

myspace.com/blackrosepdx

4038 N Mississippi Ave.

Tues-Sat 11am-6pm

> Bus #4

This little anarchist bookstore/freestore/library/resource center

spend

final price

Oregon has no sales tax.

is invaluable, no matter what your feelings are about the role of the government. You don't have to agree with any particular political party to appreciate free clothes, sliding scale books, and a "Do It Yourself" lending library. Plus, the Black Rose Collective offers patches, stickers, and records expressing views more convoluted, beautiful and sweet than anywhere else in the city. However, the usual problems that come with anarchy are present at this store: the place is open irregularly and full of smelly kids. (JB)

The Dollar Scholar
3343 SE Hawthorne Blvd. 503.235.2222
Open daily 10am-7pm
Bus #14

At this iconic dollar store you're encouraged to walk around and open or play with whatever you desire—like a chintzy version of a carnival fun house. You'll find low quality practical items—like tacks that break when you use them and off-brand cotton swabs—as well as random crap you don't want or need but will buy anyway. As the name implies it's all one dollar or less, including the back room, lined with books. (MB)

Goodwill
2215 W. Burnside St. 503.224.3084
Mon-Sat 9am-9pm, Sun 10am-8pm
Bus #20

The Portlander's quest for stylistic individuality results in a lot of picked-over thrift stores. This Goodwill branch is consistently the exception. The rich (but generous) neighbors have a shocking conception of what they deem "expendable." Try on a pair of Florsheims while shopping for a french press, and score the first season of "Pee-wee's Playhouse" while you're at it. (ML)

Teen Challenge
3121 NE Sandy Blvd. 503.230.1910
Mon-Fri 10am-5pm
> Bus #12

Teen Challenge is a faith-based thrift store ideal for inexpensive clothing, but less so if you're looking for cheap furniture. They offer everything in between clothes and couches at sensible prices as well. (ML)

spend

BOOKS

CopyLeft Books
833 SE Main St. #108 786.223.0512
Open daily 11am-7pm
> Bus #10, 14

CopyLeft Books is a small independent, radical bookshop gaining momentum in Portland. Their shelves are lined with numerous books all within the alternative genre. Pick a book on survivalism or socialism, counter culture or the occult. (ML)

In Other Words Women's Books and Resources
8 B NE Killingsworth St. 503.232.6003
Mon-Fri 10am-9pm, Sat 12pm-6pm
> Bus #44, 72

Touted as the "last surviving non-profit feminist bookstore in the United States," In Other Words welcomes anyone sympathetic to the cause, peddling books and zines. It's also a community hub with free weekly offerings including yoga, Spanish classes, music events, discussion groups, and "homo-robics" (aerobics geared towards homosexual participation). Most useful of all: their recently launched resource center designed to help connect people to necessities like rides and housing. Free Wi-Fi and plush couches encourage lounging. (MB)

spend

Laughing Horse Book and Film Collective

12 NE 10th Ave. 503.236.2893

Mon-Sat 11am-7pm

Bus #12, 19, 20, 70

Laughing Horse is another radical book and film collective in Portland, but this one comes without the pretense. Their collection is extensive, their hours are consistent, and the staff is friendly. The free Wi-Fi and the occasional in-store shows, which are easy to book yourself, are also worth a mention. (ML)

Powell's Books

1005 W Burnside St. 503.228.4651

Open daily 9am-11pm

Bus #20, Portland Streetcar

Powell's (City of) Books is a Portland institution. The store takes up an entire city block, with sixty-eight thousand square feet of new and used books on every conceivable subject. Thousands of people file through the aisles, up and down the stairs, with only a fraction of the traffic congestion of an actual city. A café and art gallery located within the store complete the experience. (ML)

VINYL

2nd Avenue Records

400 SW 2nd Ave. 503.222.3783

Mon-Fri 11am-8pm, Sat 10am-8pm, Sun 12pm-6pm

Bus #15, 51, Max Red/Blue Line, Oak Station

You can find real bargains at 2nd Avenue Records, if you can commit a solid day to thumb through their massive vinyl collection of every genre imaginable. (ML)

Clinton Street Records and Stereo

discogs.com/sell/list?seller=clintonstreetrecords

2510 SE Clinton St. 503.235.5323

Tues 1pm-7pm, Wed 1pm-5pm, Fri 1pm-7pm, Sat-Sun 11am-7pm

Bus #4, 10

Clinton Street Records, good friends with Mississippi Records, spend

resembles a small alleyway lined narrow wall to narrow wall with a little bit of every genre, in all conditions and at varying prices. This abundance of vinyl in such a small spot may seem overwhelming at first but it needn't be. The shop owner is immensely helpful and knows his collection. In addition, if he doesn't have what you're looking for in his possession, he'll get your contact information and find it for you. (ML)

Crossroads Music

3130 SE Hawthorne Blvd. 503.232.1767
Mon-Thurs 11am-6pm, Fri-Sat 11am-7pm, Sun 12pm-6pm
 Bus #14
Don't be fooled by this store's aesthetic, which gives off a "dad's record collection" vibe. Crossroads Music has every genre imaginable, from modern to vintage soul to rock 'n' roll—mostly used and thus affordable for the under-funded record collector. It's a consignment record shop with over thrity-five vendors selling albums, tapes, posters, and paraphernalia all at different prices and often with significant discounts and bargains. (MB)

Everyday Music

1313 W Burnside 503.274.0961
Open daily 9am-12am
 Bus #20
1931 NE Sandy Blvd. 503.239.7610
Open daily 9am-12am
 Bus #12, 19
Everyday Music has an expansive collection of vinyl, CDs and DVDs, though new items are often overpriced. The bargain bin of the vinyl selection is better than Goodwill but still on par with Goodwill's prices. (ML)

Exiled Records

4628 SE Hawthorne Blvd. 503.232.0751
Tues-Sat 11am-7pm Sun 12pm-5pm
 Bus #14
Bring an open mind to Exiled Records; while it doesn't have the biggest selection of records, the cozy shop is home to a

spend

never-ending supply of gems. The atmosphere is relaxed and the staff knows the collection inside and out. You'll find lots of great post-punk, no-wave, and noise records, alongside a tight selection of groove music. The cherry on top: discount bins that aren't filled with complete junk. (IF)

Green Noise Records
2615 SE Clinton St. 503.736.0909
Mon-Sat 12pm-7pm, Sun 12pm-5pm
         Bus #4, 10
Green Noise is the well-lit home to an obscene amount of punk records. They keep up with what's new and local, and maintain a solid stock with a wide range of prices. You could spend a few hours among the rows of cassettes and posters, without even venturing upstairs, where the collection continues. (IF)

Jackpot Records
203 SW 9th Ave. 503.222.0990
Mon-Thurs 10am-7pm, Fri-Sat 10am-8pm, Sun 11am-6pm
         Bus #20, Portland Streetcar
3574 SE Hawthorne Blvd. 503.239.7561
Same hours
         Bus #14, 75
If you're a recent transplant to the big city, but you still want to pay the prices you did at Sam Goody back home, try Jackpot Records. They also sell tickets to shows at the Doug Fir. (ML)

Mississippi Records
4007 N Mississippi Ave. 503.282.2990
Open daily 12pm-7pm
         Bus #4 Cash only
Mississippi Records has a small vinyl collection compared to those at other stores in town, but only because they don't buy crap. Their selection is varied—everything from soul, to tropcalia, to modern—and their prices are extremely reasonable. Scoring records from their bargain bin will give you a buzz for days. They also sell and repair record players, though the waiting list for this can be quite long. (ML)

99 Cent Records

2940 NE Martin Luther King Jr. Blvd. 503.679.6458

Tues-Fri 2pm-7pm, Sat 12pm-6pm

Bus #6

99 Cent Records is not the record store where you get that rush from scoring a great record at a great price, because here there are only okay records at one awesome price: ninety-nine cents. No thrills to be had—more of a small buzz from bulking up your collection with records that will neither inspire awe nor envy. For the price of a download, you can buy a pizza-sized, floppy, vinyl containing the one track that may just save your dance party. (MB)

Platinum Records

104 SW 2nd Ave. 877.335.6255

Mon-Sat 11am-7pm

Bus #12, 19, 20 Max Red/Blue, Skidmore Fountain Station

When the Ecstasy wears off, the body glitter washes away, the glow sticks fade, and you're ready to do it all again, hit up Platinum Records. They maintain a massive collection of House, Jungle, Dubstep, Dancehall, Hip Hop and Roots Reggae. And when your rave has gone viral but you don't even have lights, they can help there too. They sell the strobes, turntables, mixers and speakers to ensure that all those lollipops don't go to waste. (ML)

Record Room

8 NE Killingsworth St. 971.544.7685

Mon-Sat 12pm-10pm (7pm-10pm 21+) Sun 12pm-6pm

Bus #44, 72

When your friend dumps her boyfriend at two in the afternoon, the Florida Room doesn't open until four in the afternoon, and you need to drink away your sorrow now, enter the Record Room. This record store defines the twenty and thirty-something's only acceptable marriage: the one between records and beer. Two vices squared against one another with the only two losers being your wallet and your liver, and the only winner being your record collection. (ML)

spend

Sonic Recollections
sonicrec.com
2701 SE Belmont St. 503.236.3050
Tues-Sat 12pm-6pm
Bus #15

Sonic Recollections is a little atypical in its vinyl shopping experience. It has a strong online presence, with a digital, searchable catalogue. In fact, you'll find more in its online database than you will on the floor of the store. For that reason, it can be advantageous to search its website first, find your Coltrane original pressing, and then call the store with your title. The store will pull it and let you know when it's ready for pick up. The selection at Sonic Recollections is full of rarities and classics. The staff there know what they have, and they price accordingly. (ML)

Variety Shop
4932 SE Foster Rd. 503.775.2210
Open daily 11am-6pm
Bus #9, 14, 71

DVDs and VHS tapes of every genre and era line the walls of Variety Shop in the Powell/Foster neighborhood. The store houses a stellar collection of soul and classic rock vinyl, with prices that reflect an era long gone. (ML)

Vinyl Resting Place
8332 N Lombard Ave. 503.247.9573
Tues-Sat 12pm-6pm, Sun 11am-5pm
Bus #4, 17, 44, 75

The real scoop at this jazz and blues rarities store is the dollar bin; it's a pretty good bet for funk, disco and staples. Don't get me wrong: they've got a sizable pop/rock section, but there's nothing contemporary or especially worth the trip. I'd skip it unless you're into impeccably preserved jazz and blues records from before the Nixon administration. (JB)

CHAPTER 8

STUFF

These items are the tips and tricks to make your time in Portland that much smoother. Find out how to borrow a power saw for free, legally relieve yourself downtown and a cure for that inappropriate rash after ignoring it for two weeks didn't work. (ML)

stuff

Alternative Weeklys

Portland is home to three alternative weekly and biweekly rags: the Portland Mercury, the Willamette Week and Just Out. All of the papers are useful in their own regard. Both the Merc, as it's commonly called, and the Willamette Week cover local, topical news. The Willamette Week was first on the scene in 1974, and has a reputation for stellar investigative reporting. The Portland Mercury was founded in 2000 and has a reputation for being popular among the young Portlanders. The Merc is more known for chronicling Portland culture and the music scene. It provides a solid list of shows—big and small—happening around Portland (for a guide to the venues see page 59). The Willamette Week provides similar information but the Merc's is easier to read. The Willamette Week's redemption is the crossword penned by Matt Jones. Just Out is Portland's LGBT biweekly, serving the community since 1983. The biweekly paper's most perused section is the club and events calendar. All papers are available throughout the city in their own boxes and at a variety of restaurants and bars. (ML)

Bike Farm

305 NE Wygant St. 971.533.7428
Mon 4pm-7pm, Wed 4pm-7pm, Fri-Sun 12pm-4pm
        Bus #6, 72

The words that describe Bike Farm are the same ones that have come to define Portland culture: non-profit, volunteer-run, sustainable. Bike Farm is one such collective. They are not technically a bicycle shop, and as such, cannot perform repairs. Instead, the knowledgeable volunteers who work there guide you through the repair process. There are four different types of memberships, with the most simple being a drop-in-no-strings-attached rate of five dollars per hour. However, if you cycle inebriated or get hit by cars on a regular basis, it would make more sense to go for a one-month or even a year-long membership—both of which are priced absurdly cheap considering the access to professional tools and sound advice. (ML)

North Portland Tool Library

northportlandtoollibrary.org

2209 N Schofield Ave.

503.823.0209

Tues 5pm-7:30pm,

Sat 9am-2pm

Bus #4

The North Portland Tool Library is a happy byproduct of Portland's emphasis on community and "do it yourself" carpentry. Garden, power and bike tools are all available for loan to North Portland residents over the age of 18. If the Hollywood District is a little closer to home than the St. Johns neighborhood, try the Northeast Portland Tool Library. (ML)

Northeast Portland Tool Library

www.neptl.org

5431 NE 20th Ave. Basement of Redeemer Lutheran Church

Sat 9am-2pm

The Northeast Portland Tool Library provides a tool lending service to the Northeast residents west of 82nd Avenue that the NPTL does not. Pick tools up one Saturday and drop them off the following, but return them

Benson Bubblers

stuff

Simon Benson, one of Portland's "First Citizens," moved to Portland from the Midwest in 1880. He accumulated his wealth through logging and he funded, among other philanthropic efforts, the construction of forty constant-flow drinking fountains located throughout downtown Portland. In 1912, Benson donated $12,000 for the construction of the bubblers. He did so in order to discourage proletarian alcohol consumption—and we can all see how well that worked out. Urban lore about the copper plated quartets is false: the water is not recycled—nor is it drawn from the Willamette River—and the fountains are turned off at night, making it almost impossible for an errant citizen to use them as a bidet or shower. Furthermore, the city installed low flow heads in 2007, making the aforementioned bathing rituals even less possible (anecdotal evidence still endures). (JB)

stuff

late—and like any library—you will incur a fine. This library is ever expanding, so keep checking back. (ML)

Outside In Clinic

1132 SW 13th Ave. 503.535.3800
Mon-Fri Hours vary
Walk-in only

Bus #6, 15, 43, 45, 51, 55, 58, 68
Portland Streetcar

The almost-free health clinic at Outside In is designed for the "marginalized." At times, you may count yourself part of this faction. Priority goes to the "homeless" (the definition includes couch surfers and travelers) and those under twenty-one. But anyone under thirty with a "low-income" can get treatment for whatever ails them: general health, women's services, HIV/STD testing, psychiatry, and tattoo removal. It's a ten-dollar base fee, with a sliding scale from there, but no one gets turned away. They offer naturopathic and Chinese treatments in addition to good ol' Western Medicine. (MB)

Pc-pdx.com

The 89% of Portland residents in bands (made up statistic) leads to a plethora of shows available on any given night. The over-supply of entertainment and general lack of demand leads to very competitive prices, meaning that these shows are usually free or very near there. Scoping out the local talent—a loose use of the term—can best be achieved by visiting pc-pdx.com, a thorough list of venue shows as well as the occasional house show. (ML)

Rose City Resource

Rosecityresource.org
211 NW Davis St. (hard copies available here)
The Rose City Resource offers a comprehensive list of resources available in Portland, mostly targeted to people down on their luck. The RCR lists homeless shelters, soup kitchens, healthcare services, public restrooms, rehabs, as well as free food boxes

stuff

and free clothing—very thorough and quite helpful. A new edition comes out every couple of months. (ML)

Umpqua Bank
umpquabank.com
1139 NW Lovejoy St., 1241 SW 10th Ave. and more
Mon-Fri 9am-5pm typically, Sat varies

I get made fun of constantly for this, but I visit my bank daily. When a banker at Umpqua answers the phone, he's paid to say, "Welcome to the world's greatest bank"—well, he isn't lying. The bank's free public internet cafes (with the occasional printer and headphones), free coffee and tea, and free cookies on Friday are bound to draw you into one of their many locations. They know my name at Umpqua because their free coffee is part of my daily routine, but once you open an account, they'll learn your name too. (ML)

Wi-Fi PDX
When you're out and about in Portland—whether riding bikes or going to the International Rose Test Garden—and you need to check the Google with laptop in tow, use a wonderful service provided by Wi-Fi PDX. Text Wi-Fi and then the address to 41411. For example, "Wi-Fi NE 12th Ave and NE Glisan St." Be sure to include the street and avenue information. In seconds you'll receive a text directing you to the nearest Wi-Fi spot. (ML)

public restrooms

Chug too much coffee at Umpqua Bank and need some sweet relief? Piss here...

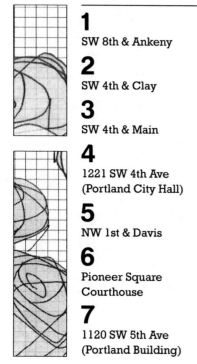

1
SW 8th & Ankeny

2
SW 4th & Clay

3
SW 4th & Main

4
1221 SW 4th Ave
(Portland City Hall)

5
NW 1st & Davis

6
Pioneer Square
Courthouse

7
1120 SW 5th Ave
(Portland Building)

8
1005 W Burnside
(Powell's Books)

9
801 S.W. 10th Avenue
(Central Library)

10
SW Taylor & SW Naito
Parkway
(Public Loo)

11
NW Glisan & NW 6th
Ave
(Public Loo)

12
SW Ash & SW Naito
Parkway
(Public Loo)

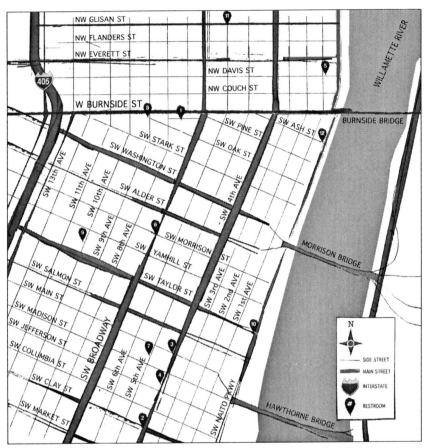

DOWNTOWN

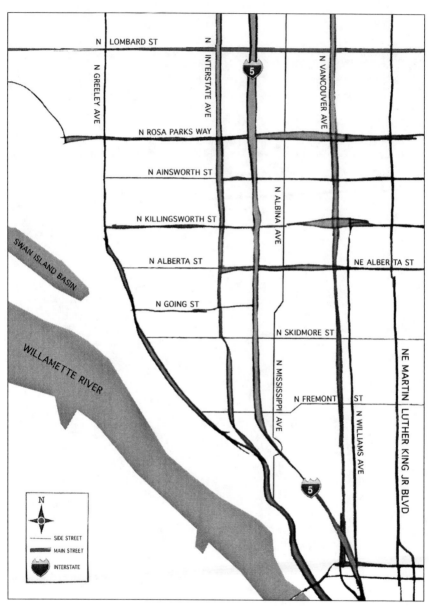

NORTH

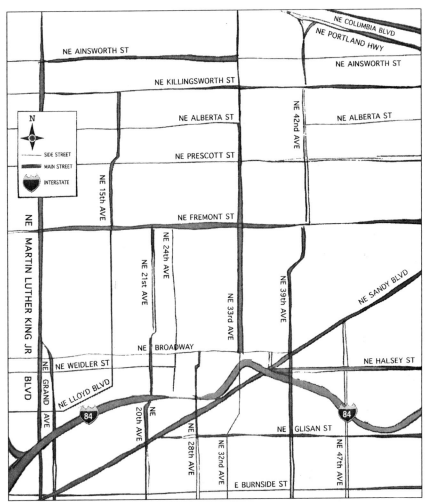

NORTHEAST

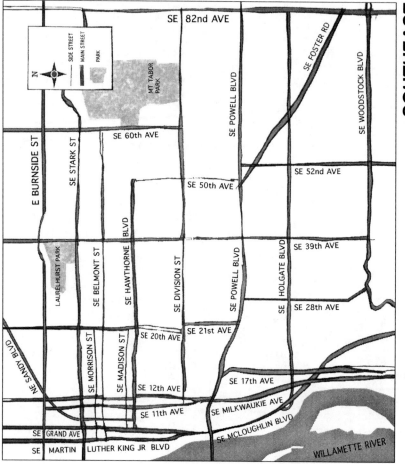

SOUTHEAST

ST JOHNS

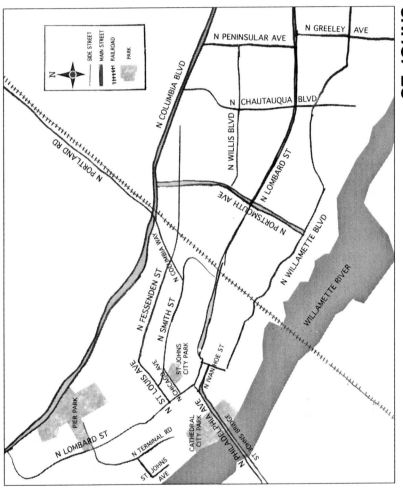

index

scratch paper

scratch paper

scratch paper

scratch paper

scratch paper

scratch paper

scratch paper

scratch paper

card scores

card scores

card scores